STRIFE
OF
DECADES

STRIFE
OF
DECADES

ODAYAM MISBAH

authorHOUSE®

AuthorHouse™
1663 Liberty Drive
Bloomington, IN 47403
www.authorhouse.com
Phone: 1-800-839-8640

Published by AuthorHouse   03/04/2013

ISBN: 978-1-4817-8656-0 (sc)
ISBN: 978-1-4817-8657-7 (e)

ABOUT THE AUTHOR

H E WAS BORN as the fifth child of a middle class family in the year 1950, in a remote countryside Odayam, near to the pilgrimage town, Varkala in the Kerala state, India. He is married and has three sons.

After completing his primary education in the nearest school, Edava High School and his graduation from Sree Narayana College, Quilon, he passed his Master of Science (M Sc) degree in Mathematics from Aligarh Muslim University in the year 1972. He is the top rank holder of that year. He also participate several competitions during that period and won several prizes. He also spent some days as a research scholar in same university.

He was a voracious reader during his college days and read not only books on his subject, but books of all branches of knowledge.

During his college days, he travelled most of the states of India to meet the people and learn the different ways of life of the vast diverse community of India. He has witnessed two communal riots in India during his stay in Northern part of India.

He came to Kuwait in 1976 and worked as teacher, accountant and on various capacities in financial sector. At present, he is working as Operations Manager of one of the prestigious financial company. After joining financial sector, he has studied for Associate of Chartered Institute of Bankers, London.

During his long stay of 35 years in Kuwait, he witnessed many historical events of this country. He was present in Kuwait during the Iraqi conquer of this country as well as the liberation of Kuwait by Allied force.

PREFACE

SEVERAL PEOPLE WHO meet me from abroad request me to tell them my experiences in Kuwait during my long stay here. Being an officer having the charge of International business relationship of a reputed company, I meet representatives of foreign companies and after the official discussion most of them spare time to enquire me about the Iraqi Occupation and my life during that period.

Because of the privation and scare during the period of unemployment and the subsequent legal battle with my previous employer for my financial losses, not only my employment benefit but also my personal funds spent for the company, I am totally perturbed. I cannot recollect the things; I even struggled to get the apt word during my conversation, a situation very similar to Alzheimer's disease. I am totally sick, physically and mentally.

I confined myself in a small room and spent most of the time in bed. Many days, I thought I might die there and my remains would decay without the knowledge of others.

This symptom persisted with full severity in the first days of my career in the new company, which affected my performance. I decided to find a way to escape from this gruesome situation. I started recollecting events and write it in a paper. First it is a tiresome job, gradually I pick up. Thus this book is born.

First up all, I must thank my new employer, Mr. Adeeb Ahmed for bearing with me in my convalesce time and providing me with moral and financial support.

During my crisis, many people stood with me. I should specially mention Mr. Ajith who considers me as a brother and helps me in his full capacity.

I thank my wife, children and siblings who rendered all kind of support to me during my difficulties.

CHAPTER 1

1990 August 2

A very hot summer day.

I got up from a small snap after the early morning fijr prayer. It was 6:30 morning, but I have to hurry up to reach my work before 7:15. Air conditioner was cooling the room throughout the night and chilled me. I moved my blanket and switch off the A/C. A bath in the warm water with sandal soap made me vibrant. Enjoying the pleasant smell of sandal, I consumed my favorite Indian breakfast dish, Dosa with a glass of water and a cup of black tea.

Dressed in light yellow shirt and black pants, I got out of the flat holding the small valet containing my office cabin keys and a small kerchief used to wipe out the sweat during my small journey to my work place. I had to roam for fifteen minutes between the tall buildings to reach the office from my residence.

A small four storied building in the middle of several sky scrapers was my work place. It is a cute building partly covered by white Italian marble and rest by glass wall, where the oldest private financial institution is functioning. Born on the first days when people settled this part of the oasis in the beginning of seventeenth century due to continued drought in the Central Arabia and grown healthy when this place became a centre for spice trading between India and Europe, this institution became a major player in the financial market in Kuwait.

When I reached the lift, my neighbor, Aleem, a pretentious bank officer was waiting there cursing the bad climate. He was happy to get a listener for his achievements and gossip, in single minute he talked several things mostly about the vices of his neighbour. After reaching the ground floor, he accompanied me till the ITC building where his car was parked. He stopped me there and talked about that building which rises like a tower joining two six storey old buildings of same shape and structure. He lectured to me the internal and external beauty of that tall 12 storey building. Already dishearten by is stupid talk in shrill voice, I thought it was prognostic of some bad omen.

Avoiding scourge of sun, I walked through the shadow on the western side of the buildings till I reached the Mubarakiya side of city, where the 'heritage market' lay like the compartments of a passenger train. These are shacks with Iron beams and wooden roof and cement brisk walls, stand as a memorial of the generation old way of merchant shops in this country.

In front of one of the shops, five people are surrounding a big tray, chewing the local bread known as quboos with teas in instikan, small glasses. Mr. Abu Hamed, a sweet merchant was one among them. While passing them I heard the word 'Fadel", the invitation for joining them, which I rejected with thanks.

I crossed the next building and reached my work place. The watchman, a very tall and fatty Sudanese greeted me saying

"Assalamu Alakum". I responded Wa Allaiku Massalam" and entered the building.

I unzipped my valet, took the cabin key and opened the cabin.

I throw the valet on my office table and rushed the Reuters screen to open it.

Daily morning I start my work by updating the currencies transaction rates in the computer system of the company. For this I check the rate screen of the Reuters for which we pay a plenty of money as subscription fees.

I gazed the screen where the buying and selling rate of various currencies are splashing and changing with the updates. In the top row of the screen the rate of Sterling pounds was shown followed by Deutsche Mark, Swiss Franc, French Franc, Italian lire etc until it ends with Japanese Yen.

I moved my eyes from the top towards bottom, beneath the bottom row; the horrifying news was flickering: "Iraq Invaded Kuwait".

I sat on the chair numbed till I regained my consciousness. Nobody was around to share my feelings.

I called the chairman of the company for instruction. An obese man, who usually talked with heavy breathing sound, spoke to me with more strain in a frightening voice:

"Close the company indefinitely. Leave the place quickly"

I picked the phone to advise the branches one by one. When I advised the sixth branch I saw my colleague Mr. Nadeem Ahmed was entering the hall. I spoke to him as if he was aware of the incidence, but he fainted before I complete my talk.

He was a man in his sixties, undergone a heart surgery recently and were convalescing

A calm and quiet man, residing just two kilometers away from the company knew only one route to reach the office that was the sea road passing through the front side of the Seif Palace, the official Palace of Kuwait Ruler.

Other workers were also come up.

All were afraid and spell bound. With the help of some of them, I completed the call to the branches and was ready to leave the office.

When I closed my cabin only three were left; me, Mr. Nadeem Ahmed and the accountant Mr. Salem Ansari.

Mr. Nadeem Ahmed told me "Please come with me to show another route to my house. Mr. Salem agreed to drive my car because I am too scared to drive"

Salem asked me to accompany him because he did not know Nadeem's residences.

I yielded to their request and agreed to accompany them.

We exited from the building.

Nadeem said "See the road is empty at this peak hour"

I responded "Still some shops are open. They may not hear the news".

Nadeem's car was parked near the beach road, which stood as a divider between his car and Seif Palace.

He was too afraid to go there.

He said "Better we leave the car there, Insha Allah we take it another day"

Salem, in his mid thirties asked the car key. Nadeem expressed his fear and was reluctant to hand over the key.

Salem feels as an insult to his age and persuades Nadeem to give the keys to him. At last the fear of the old man surrendered to the courage of the young man.

I and Nadeem stood in front of the company building till Salem brought car there.

Inside the car, Nadeem sat spell bound while Salem and me were discussing the political situation of Kuwait. It took less than ten minutes to reach the residence of Nadeem and we left him and his car there. Before wading farewell Nadeem prayed for our safety as if we would never meet again.

Nadeem's residence is very near to the Dasman Palace, residence of the present Amir and all the movements there are visible from his flat. We see two tanks are moving towards to palace.

In the ordeal Salem forgot his car which was parked near to our company. We decide to walk there and he promises give a lift to me to my residence.

When we reached the main road we heard the sound of the first shot from the Dasman palace.

Salem joked "Nadeem may die from fear hearing the sound".

But fear was slowly gripping us and we walked some distance without uttering any word.

We reached near the Grand Mosque, and saw the first Iraqi soldier. When we moved further, a huge number of soldiers were visible in front of the Sief palace. We both were too scared to move further. Regaining his courage Salem told me "Let us part away here. I take my car and go to the other direction"

After leaving him, I walked ten feet when I heard an immense sound that break my ear drum and shook my feet. I turn my face back to the palace side, and felt like hundreds of lighting and thunder were erupted from there.

Hurrying to my residence, I chose the shortest route. The heat of sun subsided to a level lower than my inside fire. I crossed the underground passage at Darwasa Abdulrazak and reached main road going to the next city Salmiya. A plane suddenly appeared in the sky, rounding in short circumference of the capital city.

Moving further, I reached in front of the International Turnkey System (ITS) building. Something is flying toward the plane with a horrifying sound. It lost its aim and fell in the open ground behind the ITS building and burst shaking the whole area.

I just passed that building, a cracker sound is heard from behind. The wall clad marble tiles of that marvelous building were pouring to the ground with raising the mud.

Thank God, I escaped marvelously by a split of a second.

Closing my eyes, I moved away from that site and my head hit on the pillar of the next building. Fearing that the building would collapse I run out of the corridor to the main road.

I stood in the road side in front of my residential building, indecisive to enter the building or stay in open space.

Then I heard the husky sound of some military vehicles approaching to my side. Without hesitating, I rush to my flat.

I was staying as a paying guest with a family from a village only 12 kilo meters away from my home town in India. Two of their grown up children are married and settled in India. The Father, Mother and the youngest son are staying there packing their things to settle in India because the father, the only bread earner of the family got the retirement notice from the airlines company he was working for the last 32 years.

When I entered the flat, I saw our neighbors Mr. Mathew, Mr. David and their families filled the sitting room. They are all eagerly waiting for me to know the news I read from the Reuters.

Kuwait Television is broadcasting an Arabic movie, which no one listening; all were expecting some news at any time.

I put only one leg inside the room, I heard the chorus "Misbah has come".

Mr. David came forth and asked me "Tell me what is the Reuters News".

All were desperate when I told them that I left the office after reading the first splash news.

I narrated to them my ordeal which helped to mitigate their desperation.

Suddenly the topic slipped to our own life:

Head of the family, Mr.Rafeeq told "I am the most unfortunate man in the world"

David responded 'why?'

Rafeeq replied "You don't know that I am retiring next week. I planned several things with the retirement benefits. I have no other income for rest of my life"

Mathew, who is financially and physically sound, told "You have grown up children; they will take care of their father and mother"

The father answered "What guaranty? Who will support the youngest?"

David cried "What about me? I booked my ticket in tomorrow's flight to go USA for the surgery there"
"I may die in this country; my body may be buried without sermon"

There was a brief pause after hearing the word 'die'.

He is one among the few Indian who came to Kuwait, prior to Independence.
After retirement from Kuwait Fire service, David joined a fire equipment supplier company only for the residence permit to stay with his wife, and his young children.

He married here to a lady three times bigger than him because of the scarcity of Indian women in Kuwait at that time. Their four children, three boys and one girl, were born and brought up here. He did not visit his native place for more than a quarter of a century and he had no contact with his poor relatives in India.

His two sons went to USA for higher studies and married two nurses and settled there. His daughter is engaged to a friend of the boys and soon or later she will also migrate to USA. His youngest son also applied for a student visa to that country.

Thereafter, he had an ambition to go and die in that marvelous land. He used to say USA is dear to him like Israel to Jews.

Hearing his prayers, God gave him a chance. He is inflicted by stones in his kidney. Although there is severe pain, he does not want to meet any doctor in Kuwait. Only doctor from USA will be allowed to touch his body.

Rukiya, the wife of Rafeeq broke the silence "Misbah is lucky. He sends his wife to India last week'

Annama, the wife of Mathew continued the conversation "what will be condition if she is here. Her delivery is in the next month. Not one but two children"

That worried me reminding my family. I planned to go to India and stay with wife at the delivery time and my leave application was approved and I booked the ticket. How can I go now?

My eyes filled with tears, to hide it I entered my room and changed my dresses.

When I returned to the gathering, Mathews said "My brother may call me. He will be worried if the phone is not attended. I am leaving now"

Mathew and family left.

The wife of David, Mrs. Janky nicknamed as Jumbo, told to her husband "Achchaya, we will also go home. The children may call us"

No one uttered a word for some time and that silence was biting our heart.

Now it is time for the noon (DHOHER) prayer and I go to the wash room for ablution.

CHAPTER 2

A FTER THE PRAYER I sat in the prayer mat, read the Quran for some time.

Heavy sound from the side of the Dasman Palace pierced my ears.

My head sunk with the fears and I lay down in the bed covering the whole body by blanket.

I closed my ears with my hands and lay on the bed for a lengthy period.

Now the noise subsided, I thought one of the parties surrendered. Which one?

Most probably, Kuwaiti.

Kuwaitis are enjoying their life with all available happiness while Iraqis lost their wealth and life for fighting with Iran for decades.

Kuwaiti boys are born and brought up in the fullest luxury, fully maintained by this welfare nation.

Kuwait was supporting Iraq by wealth and weapon all these days.

One night in year 1980, I was traveling in a car with a friend and stuck in a traffic signal for more than 2 hours. Traffic police car barricaded the road.

Hundreds of tanks and thousands of other armed vehicles were moving in the street as Kuwait contributions to Iraq war against Iran. Coffer of Iraq was filled with Kuwait Wealth.

If you give the milk to a snake it will reciprocate by a bite on your hand that is the natural truth.

Now, how can I escape from here and join my family?

We are expecting our first child next month; the gynecologist told us my wife is carrying twin children.

I know that my family is very much worried hearing the news.

I got up from the bed and went to the telephone. No one is picking phone at my house. Where is she?

After four five attempts, I rang to my sister's house, very near to mine. My niece attended my call;

She said "Mamachy, they all went to the hospital"

Hearing the world hospital I interrupted her "What is wrong? Why all are in Hospital"

She replied "Nothing serious. Mami's BP level has gone up and we decide to admit her in the hospital"

She calls me Mamachi means uncle and my wife Mami, uncle's wife in our language.

She continued "Hearing the news about Kuwait, she is very upset; she knows that the war field is very near to your office and home".

I told "Inform all that I am very safe and will reach there very soon". And I hung up the receiver.

My wife stayed with me nearly 10 months and left Kuwait because all suggested sending her to get good care at home. Moreover, these the first delivery in my wife house after a period of 24 years when my wife was born.

If we consider the wife joint family, there are four grandmothers, they have three daughters but one of them has children, my wife and her sister. My wife sister is barren, which is blamed customary to the woman. Thus, all want to celebrate the arrival of the first in the fourth generation.

Moreover, nobody is here to take care of the mother and children during my absence. Hence, I send my wife to India.
I sat in front of the television hearing Quran verses for a while.

The Lady of the house brought some food

We have food enough for three days, if we tighten our stomach, we can extend it to one week.

After a pause, she said "Rest is with Allah".

She is a 2nd degree diabetic patient pulling her life with half medicine and half controlled food.

I asked her "Do you have medicine?"

She replied "for 20 days, I may reduce the dosage to avail till I reach my home. What is the use of medicine if there is no food"

By home meant her house in India. Everyone starts thinking to travel to their native place.

But How?

Her hospitality is very famous in our community and any one comes that house enjoyed her delicious food. She always stores a very high quantity of food items, but since she is planning to leave the country for good, she does not stock any food recently.

Her husband and son also joined us for the food and I ate breads with little chicken curry.

I heard a rasping sound near to the Public Commercial Centre building in front of my residence. I peeped through the window. One trailer lorry, containing goods was parking there.

The driver got down and made a search. All shops were closed. He sat on the parapet of the building for sometime sipping water from a bottle.

After taking my evening prayer, I again looked through the window, that person vanished, leaving the truck there.

Two three persons are seen in the street, otherwise the street is empty.

I found my recourse in the Holy Quran nearly two hours.

Around 5:00 PM Mr. Mathew came with his family to share their agony with us. This time they were worried because his sister in law did not return from the last night work so far.

She is a nurse working in the AMIRI hospital in the sea side near to the Dasman Palace, went for night duty last night. All the telephones of the Hospital are blocked and the outside contact of the 'inmates' are not allowed. Only the patients, doctors and supporting staff are allowed and all caretakers of the patients were thrown out of the office.

Since no staff has reported for duty in the morning and all doctors, nurses and supporting staff worked in the night shift were ordered to continue their work.

Iraq Military took over the control of this Hospital. No one was allowed to enter the hospital compound. The brother of Mr. Mathew went there to know the whereabouts of his wife and he was sent back by an army person pointing gun towards him.

Then, every one remembered Sumaya, a 2 year cute baby of the neighboring Pakistani family. She was watching the excavator digging the ground from her balcony and fell down. As a miracle, she escaped with only small injuries and was admitted to the same hospital. Her mother Asma, was staying with her.

The subject of our conversation slipped to Sumaya,

Rukiya started 'it is the 3rd day I am missing my girl, I am much worried of her"

Her husband said "she is very entertaining, she talks Malayalam, also she sings song"

'When I go to kitchen, she will stay in the visitors room viewing the TV, She never behaved mischievously" Rukiya said.

Annamma said 'whenever I come here, she calls me aunty and talks to me without stop. Have u heard anything today"

Rukiya said "There are a lot of men there, so I do not go there. I am anxious to know about her"

"let us go there" Annamma said.

"Better u both ladies go there and enquire to her mother" Rafeeq said, exhibiting his nature of aliening from labors and non office workers.

Rukiya and Annamma went there to gather the information

All members of that family behave funereally that made these ladies sob. The military order the mother to get out of the place immediately. Looking backwards, she rushed to the lift and before she enters the lift she saw her child was thrown to the corridor. She moved toward Sumaya to take her, but the military man did not allow her to move to that side.

Thereafter no news about that prodigy is heard.

When everyone goes to work or school, Rukiya is alone in the home, idle and isolated. This young girl flies like butterflies around her during these hours and learn the vernacular language of Rukiya. She speaks Malayalam along with her mother tongue Urdu. She learned two languages before attaining the age of 2.

She is the eight of the nine children of her mother. Her mother, a 29 year old village girl from the outskirt of Rawalpindi, is always busy in the kitchen in addition to looking after her old mother in law and her youngest 4 month old son. She cooks the snacks for her family restaurant in addition to the milk and cereals for her younger children.

Her most tiresome work is massaging her mother in law daily with a full bottle of olive oil. Her mother in Law, Atheekka is only 58 year old women full of energy, but act as if she has pain in her whole body. Even her son, Salman is much worried of her, if she spends her life only for eating the most delicious

foods without doing any work, she may soon become ill. She never cares the children and even curses if they do something naughty.

On the other hand, Salman's Father Khader is a very beautiful and loving person, very much loves his grand children and others. Like his son, he spends day and night for their business.

Salman first married to his cousin, Jouhara, the daughter of his mother's brother. Unable to bear the abuse in her husband family she returned to her father's house taking her two children. His mother tried to bring her back in vain, only because she was the most hated person in that house by her daughter in law.

The mother in law has her own story, the story of hardship suffered in her husband house. This is the mentality of vast majority of ladies in Indian Subcontinent. They forget their miseries as daughters in law when they become mothers in law. They do not think that their daughter in law may hate them similarly they do to their mother in law.

Thereafter, Salman married to the eldest of the eight daughters of a cook in a village restaurant owned by a relative of him. She was fourteen only at the time of the marriage. Her father has nothing to pay him as dowry, no gold, no land. So she became a slave there.

Her husband gives less attention to the wife and children, but his father take care of them,

She can not go back to her family like Jouhara because of the poverty at home. She stays with her husband to give birth to a child each year.

When she put the suggestion that she will cook the snack for the restaurant for a small earning for her personal needs, her father in law refused first, saying that she may not get enough time to look after the children. But, Atheekka has another idea.

She insisted to dismiss two cooks from the restaurant and hand over their duties to Asma, to save the wages of them.

To avoid a quarrel Khader agreed, but, without the knowledge of his wife, he used to send money to the father of Asma, and spent for her personal expenses.

Khader has four more children, one woman and three men, all are happily living in Pakistan. They are jointly maintaining the family business in Pakistan. Their wives jointly want to keep away their mother in law.

But each one of them visits their parents with wife and children once in a year to take their shares from Kuwait Business and purchases gold and other luxuries.

One or two weeks they are treated as guests. They will return before Atheekka changes her mood and shows her real colour.

Soumaya is the youngest of the two girls, among the nine children of Asma. When her month is busy in the kitchen, she goes to her grand mother to play with her. Their meeting starts in friendly notes which gradually turn into abusing and beating. To avoid this Asma bring her to our flat to spend her time until her elders come back from school.

Rukiya treated Soumaya as her own child. She is very eager to know the condition of Soumaya.

The atmosphere is thick with agony.

Mathew who was initially not moved by the incident now started creaming like a child. Now, he starts estimating his losses, his highly remunerated job, his wife's earnings, bank deposits, his and his wife's retirement benefits etc.

Some felt sorrow for him, others happy because of jealousy.

Every one throw their problems on the floor, every one's heart burst with agony and in the end rejoiced thinking their losses are less than others.

It was time for the prayer at the sun set; I stood up and said "Now God only can save us. I am going to pray to him".

Annama said "we may also go home and read the bible"

CHAPTER 3

TOTALLY DISILLUSIONED I spent most of the time in the bed and prayer. Laying in the bed and thinking about my future. I cannot find out a clear plan to spend my rest of the life.

My mind started to read the chronicle of events in my life.

My disappointment swings me to the bottom of the ocean of agony. I felt I am a fallen angel.

I recollected the events that lead me to the present condition from a research scholar at a reputed University; Misfortune or foolishness?

After graduation from Sree Narayana College Quilon, I applied for admission in the same college for Masters Degree. There was a delay from receiving their call, I approached Aligarh Muslim University, Aligarh, Utter Pradesh which is nearly 2700 Kilo meters away from my house. There is no direct train from my place to this city where there is no Air Port at that time. First I have to go to New Delhi and then catch another train to Aligarh.

After three complete days of train journey I reached this educational city. There were few students from my locality to this University, which is established by Sir Syed, a prominent social reformer. Among them my co-brother was there and he helped me in the initial stage.

The day after my arrival in Aligarh, I got a letter from my house which was sent to me in the care of address of my co-brother informing that my admission for MSc in my previous college is approved. I decided to stay in Aligarh, because of its prominence as the biggest University in Asia and the many facilities offered to the students.

After the college hours, I will spend my time to the library for reading not only my academic books, but of all branches of knowledge. I rarely go out of the University campus, most of my outing is to the nearest snack bar, where I ate Punjabi Samosa and drink, sweat lessy. This is the only Hindu shop in the Muslim Dominated area of Aligarh.

We can say Aligarh is a twin city although there is no demarcation separating the Muslim residence area and Hindu residence area. There is always communal tension in the bordering area for a long time.

In the year 1971, the Bangladesh Liberation war has started and India had interfered in the conflict. Surveillance War planes round the big cities of New Delhi and Agra, which cross the sky of Aligarh during night time. Every one stayed inside their residence during the night time and never went to the city center for shopping or seeing the movies.

The war ended in December of that year, but the aftermath of the war is very much worrying.

There was an election for Indian parliament; the ruling Congress party put a Muslim as its candidate, while a Hindu, who was an aspirant of that post, contested an Independent candidate. The money and power stood with the Muslim, hence the Hindu candidate had only one drum card, the communal card, which he played well. He incited the communal feeling of the people for his own gain and finally a communal conflict erupted.

That day, myself and two others from my locality were in city area when the riot and looting started. We were inside a textile when the rioters attack the next shop of Muslim, the shop owner, a Hindu asked us to hide inside the fitting room. We were very much scared because the intension of the shop owner, who had an Ardhachandra Tilak in his forehead evidencing that he is a Vyshnava Hindu, was not clear, we doubt that this obese man wearing saffron Kurta was blocking us from escaping. We noticed that his face became red due to anger and fear.

From inside of the fitting room, we heard the closing sound of the shop front door and he wished the looters "Ram Ram". We opened the door of the fitting room little and peeped through it. The front shutter is half lowered and his legs were visible in front of the shop.

When they left, he directed us to go the left side and cross the road to Muslim side of city. We thanked him and crossed the road.

We saw a man laying a pool of blood, begging for help and no one dared to assist him. There are friendship and co-operation between the shop owners of the area without any religious discrimination, but the seed of hatred is sowed now.

When we reached the Muslim area, the people are gathering there to protect themselves or attack others. We were afraid when they came running towards us holding swords and iron bars. One of us, Hasan wished them "Assalamu Alaikum'.

After their reply, one person asked us our names. Because of the fear and nervousness Basheer hesitated to reply, which roused their suspicion.

Rising his sword one of these men asked Basheer "Tell the Kalima"

Since he was very scared, he said a Surrah of Quran, instead of Kalima.

"Does he say the Kalima", someone was asking him from the nearest building.
"Yes, he said Kalima" the replied by the first person,
May be he does not know the Kalima, the basic thing of Islam, because most of the religious fanatics are totally ignorant of the religion.

"Show them the safest route" the second person said.

Four persons followed us till the end of the city centre and asked us to go quickly to the campus.

We tried to get a taxi or auto rickshaw to return to our college hostel, but no one helped us. Everyone is running to save their own life. We ran nearly 3 Kilo meters from that place till we reach the University campus.

I was totally exhausted and directly went to the bed. There were few students in the hostel because many had left to home for the holidays after the midyear examination. I wake up from the bed hearing the loud conversation between three of the inmates of the hostel. They were discussing the way to travel out of Aligarh because the hostel would be closed from the next day. I joined them and explained my ordeal in the previous night; fear and tear were seen in my face.

I packed my things and wait in front of Sir Syed Hall, the hostel where I was staying, for the Military vehicle. My co-brother and others from my native place went home after the midterm examination and I stayed in Aligarh only to spend my time in the library.

In the military truck I met Ismail, whose native place is a village 15 kilometers away from my place. He is studying for Masters Degree in English Language and Literature and we regularly meet in the library. He was rejoiced that he got a companion till the end of the journey.

Army is deployed throughout the city and there is no vehicle in the street other than armed force trucks. All the shops were closed and no person is seen in the street.

The condition in the Railway station is entirely different; it is filled with people, even no place even to thumb a nail. With great difficulty, we reached the queue for the ticket, which is very long, with several hairpin bends.

Suddenly Ms. Sarojani, one of the classmates of Ismail approached him asking his assistance to reach Madras, she is very scared and does not have the money required to purchase a ticket. Ismail has only few funds with him which is scarcely enough for his own expenses. He asked me whether I can spare some money for her, which I agreed. We stand in the queue for more than three hours to reach the booking counter and got the ticket in the ordinary compartment of the train.

Still there is two hours for the train, so we sat on the corner of the flat form I offered a cup of tea and a cake, because we could not get anything until we reach New Delhi. While sipping the tea we see Mary Vyse, another classmate of Ismail coming towards us.

She came to the railway station with her sister, but her sister left her in the station and went with her lover, leaving this poor girl alone among the violent condition. She also asks our assistance to reach Madras; she is ashamed as well as afraid by the action of her sister. After she joined our company, her sister came to us with the grief that she got only two first class tickets to New Delhi and she cannot keep Mary with her during the journey.

We enter the train with all our luggage, Mary has more luggages which we understand that she is carrying the luggage of her sister also, giving them more comfort and enjoyment.

All the seats in that compartment are occupied by Army men who are returning from the war field. We four are the only civilians in that compartment. They are enjoying their life which is saved by the mercy of God. drinking, dancing, singing. When they saw the two ladies, they started harassing and trying to touch the bodies of the frightened girls and myself and Ismail had to protect them.

The train reached New Delhi after 2 ½ hours journey, around 12:30 Midnight. Since our luggage is kept in the corridor near to the door and we are standing, we are able to get down from the train before the army man.

Still we have three days journey, we tried in vain to book reservation of seats in the sleeping coach. Mary's sister and lover arranged seat bribing heavily the ticket examiner through the railway porter. There also Mary is avoided and left penniless since we are four and seats are not available even if we bribe, we take the ticket for the ordinary compartment and decide to bear all the suffering.

To our misfortune the ordinary compartment in Grand Trunk Express is also filled with Army men, although they have separate compartment. There are too many soldiers to accommodate in one compartment, so they occupied the nearest compartment also. Since they are coming from battlefield they are enjoying all available facilities. We spend our time standing and sitting on our luggage, until the next day morning, when the some of the soldiers got down the train at a railway station in Andhra Pradesh. We got two seats where the ladies can sit and drowse and we both boys sat over our luggage comfortably.

One of the soldiers who are aged around 55 years is from Nagarcoil, the same place of Sarajoni and he makes arrangements to give that full seat to the ladies for sleeping.

He said to Sarojani "I have daughter of your age and I am a relative of Kannan, the village assistant in your area"

She replied "I know Kannan because of my uncle is the village officer there. I will come with you. I will telephone my uncle to receive me at station."

Then Mary said "You don't worry about your journey. My brother is working in Madras and he will meet us at the railway station. We will go to his house, refresh and continue our journey."

In the next stop three more soldiers got down and we got enough space to sit and sleep. We had only two solid meals in two days and ordered four vegetarian meals from railway catering.

We reached Madras, unloaded the heavy luggage and stand in the flat farm. The soldier said farewell and left. After a while, Mary's brother came to receive her, along with her sister and Shahid. They took her luggage and left without saying a single word to us. Sarojani made a pained look to her classmate, who promised to arrange her onward journey to Nagarcoil. The soldier who is willing to assist her also left. Her train will start from the next flat form in fifteen minutes. I take her ticket while she and Ismail are searching that soldier. She travelled on the same train along with that soldier.
When the train started, we came out of the railway station and telephoned to her uncle from the nearest booth to meet her at the Nagercoil station.

Now we have to go to Egmore station, wherefrom the train to our place is going. Fortunately, our journey is comfortable, and we reached home in the next day evening.

After a short stay at home, I return to Aligarh to continue my studies and completed my post graduation in the year 1972. Thereafter I stayed there with the intention of doing my PhD and registered under the guidance of Prof. Abdul Mohsin.

My mother became sick and I came back home in the year 1973 to meet her. I planned to go back to Aligarh within two months, unfortunately it was delayed because her convalesce prolonged a long period. It was a time, when the work of the house for my eldest sister is continuing.

In year 1974 I purchased five bag of Cement from an authorized dealer when there was control for cement purchase. I did not obtain a permit because the quantity was very low.

It took more than two years to be acquitted by a court. There end my carrier.

I am mentally very much perturbed and I wish to be away from that place for some time.

The professor, who was guiding me in my research, migrated to a foreign country and my research fellowship was cancelled

My childhood friend, Musadiq, came to our native place from Dubai on vacation. We enjoyed his holidays together, watching movies, visiting places and people. One day, I explained to him my ambition to stay away from this place.

Musadiq asked me 'why cannot you come to Dubai? I will arrange a Visa for you"

I enquired" What will be the expenses?"

He answered "My friend Sameer is visa trader. He can arrange one for you. As you as I reach Dubai, I will write to you"

He exited me saying the life in Dubai and how educated people are treated there. He end up saying "if you work there two years, you can earn enough money to go to Europe for higher studies'

I fell flat hearing his words and decided to go to Dubai. I applied for passport the very next day.

At that time a lot of people are going to Arabian Gulf countries to work and my mind turned to that direction.

I got the letter one week after he reached Dubai in which he wrote that he had arranged the visa for me, which cost INR 5,000. He also wrote to hand over the money to his brother as early as possible.

INR 5000 is a very big sum which is enough to buy 2 acres of land in our area. But this did not discourage me and I submitted this matter to my family for discussion.

My eldest sister said "We are always worrying about Vaheed. Now you also started the same thing"

My father advised me "if you pay INR 5000 as capitation fee to any aided college, you can be a lecture, with government salary. Even after retirement, you will get pension which is enough for your living."

Mother takes the matter emotionally and started crying.

I tried very hard to convince them that a short stay in Gulf will rejuvenate me and free me from all my present problems.

As advised me I paid INR 5,000 to the brother of Musadiq and wait for months. After several months, he informed me that my brother Vaheed discourages him from taking my visa and he would arrange my higher studies in Europe, which I was untruc according to my knowledge. I asked Musadiq to return the INR

5,000 I paid him. There was no response from him for my several letters. After two years, his brother returned INR 4,000 and the remaining is not yet paid

Hearing this news, a close relative of mine approaches my family offering a visa for me for a payment of INR 4,000, half of it to be paid immediately and rest when the visa is ready. Thus we lost another INR 2,000.

In the year 1975, Machcha, my eldest brother in law and his friends of Malaysia went for Haj from Kuala Lumpur and returned to India. On their journey to India they met Asmabi an old servant of Machcha's family at the Mumbai airport.

She said "Now I am working in Kuwait as an Aya of a school. my two brothers are also in Kuwait working as officers of a very big company."

One of Macha's friend, Abdul Salam asked her "can your brother arrange a visa for my relative"
She answered "of course, he can any numbers'
He asked her "how much you want me to pay?"
She said 'After checking with him, I will inform you'

Later she informed him that they need INR 10,000 and she had no financial benefit on it.

That visa is received within 10 days after exchange of the passport details and money.

Abdul Salam arranged another visa for a dowry payment for the bridegroom of his niece.

Sooner Visa has become the most attractive dowry items in our place, especially for unemployed youth. Unlike, Muslims of other part of the world, in some areas girl's family is paying the dowry as the prominent custom of other communities. Sometimes the personal merits of the bridegroom are not considered for the dowry amount, but the family prestige is major family. The measurement of "family prestige" is fictitious and not based on any particular norm. In many cases, the wealth of the previous generation is the major factor, although presently they are penniless.

Machcha travelled to India in January 1976 to celebrate his annual vacation, when my problem is the major topic in my family. He promised me to arrange the visa through Abdul Salam.

Abdul Salam demanded 2000 INR additional for the visa, which, everyone knows, is his commission. Macha paid him that amount and asked me to wait a few days.

After several days of waiting, I reached Kuwait on 16th April 1976, a country where I have no acquaintance. Still my ambition to complete my research was haunting me. I decided to spend few days here until my mind is prepared for it.

There were 7 another persons who received the visa from Asmabi through Abdul Salam. Some of them as illiterate and others had very low education. Three of them are fishermen and the remaining has no previous working experience in Kerala, a place where the employment chances are very rare. But to my astonishment, all these persons got visas for employment in companies, while I got a domestic visa to work in the house where Asmabi was working cleaner. One of the unemployed got a visa of doctor while all the previous fishermen got the visa as Engineering. It was time, the qualification of people is not considered for issuing visas.

To my dismay, I came to know that the brother of Asmabi was working as driver in a private trading firm and he was spending his rest times in brothel. Entirely different from the information given by Asmabi, she and her brothers live in the lowest standard level of life as prostitute, pimps and bootleggers.

My first struggle here is to find a shelter and then food. The agent who arranged the visa for me threw me in a shed, already occupied by eleven persons. A side of that shed is separated by two bed sheets switched together, hanging like a curtain. A cot is put there used by Asmabi and her paramour, a temporary arrangement during their stay in Kuwait. They are the actual tenants of that shed where nine young men including the grown up son of that person, were also staying. I joined that group as the 12th member.

For food, that lady will bring something from the house she is working and the man also bring from his work place, a restaurant. All are mixed in a big tray all the nine rounded it and eat eagerly. This is the only food they receive.

When I sit with them for food, I nauseate, hence could never eat anything from that tray.
There was a very small balance left with me from the small amount brought from India as travel expenses. I will buy an Irani Qubus, which is tasty and can fill my stomach with a mouth full of water. Fortunately, water dispenser are kept in front of several building for public, which filled by stomach even without solid food.

Do not think that these are free, they are charged Kuwait Dinar twenty for each month per head. A nice investment, the total expenditure is Kuwait Dinars twenty, paid as rent of the shed.

Fortunately, I found a temporary job as a school teacher very soon to gain enough money to change my residence to a better place. By this time my visa formalities are completed.

A relative of a person, who travelled with me, came to our shelter on the next Friday, the weekly holiday in Kuwait. He was carrying the English Newspaper, Arab Times, published in the previous day in which there was an advertisement for teacher's job. I telephoned to the school and arranged an interview in the next day.

Next day I woke up early and took of my ration of one bucket of water for the whole day and went to the toilet. A roommate, Salahuddin, who is working in a restaurant run to occupy the toilet before me, hence I returned to the shelter waiting for him. I opened my bag and took out the only new pair of dresses because the two set of dresses used by me a very dirty the interview. When that man came out, I entered the toilet and finished my morning works with the small quantity of water.

When I return to my room, my new dresses are missing and one person told me that Salahuddin gone out wearing that dress. I went to the school wearing the dirty cloth, thinking that the interviewer may have a bad impression for my dress code.

The location of the school is given as the first building if we go to sea side from bus terminal of Route No.2. I took another occupant of our shed, Abu Baker, the son in law of Asmabi with me because he knows the place. We reached the bus terminal in the opposite direction and walked to the sea side. There are several buildings, but nothing is a school. We walked more than two Kilometers and finally asked on Indian. He said the school is more than 3 kilo meters away and near to the bus terminal in the other side. Other Indian, who goes that direction give us a free lift and drops us in front of the school.

It is a school run by Christian Machineries, and the principal is a nun. The XI standard is introduced that year and they are looking for post graduate teachers. May they could not find another, they hired me.

While I work in the school one of my old roommates, Mr.Basheer came to me and told me "Raouf Sir asks me to bring you to his residence"

I asked him "who is Raouf?"
He said 'you do not know Raouf sir, He is a big shot in Kuwait. He has arranged my job. His acquaintance with him will be much helpful to you"

Thus I met Mr.Raouf with him. When I entered Raouf's flat I felt as if I was entering a recreation club, where a lot of people sitting around two tables, playing cards. Some are sipping liquor, which is prohibited in this country.

He is one of the few people who came to Kuwait before its independence. He is born and brought up in a fishermen community and has no schooling. He joins Group Fisheries, a fishmonger company when most of the people here is engaged in fishing. He grew with the company and became its accountant, although the company employed another qualified person to manage the finance of the company.

I wait more than two hours until he attends me. After a brief introduction he told me "I can arrange a good job for you. The school management forbids one boy from my place to entire the school because of his mischievous behaviour, but they will give him attendance and allow him to sit in the examination. So, he wants a tutor to teach him all subjects. You will get a good remuneration"

He continued 'If you are willing I will talk to the parent of that boy'

I said 'Give me two days because I have a chance to get a part time job in a reputed company'

When I met, Kalam, I asked about these people. Kalam, an educated person from their locality told me "Do not go there. They are all upstarts without any educational background and moral family status."

I decided to reject this offer after Kalam narrated me their history.

But, next day Basheer told me that Raouf asked him to convey the message that he agreed with the parents of that boy to appoint me as a tutor for payment me KD 35 per month. I said to him that I was not interested in that offer. Raouf was very angry when he heard my decision.

In Kuwait, school summer vacation starts from 1 June and end in middle of August in every year, hence I have to stay idle without salaries for this period. I tried to several places for a job, and I joined Group Fisheries as a store assistant on temporary basis.

It is the time when the work of Group Fisheries is computerizing and the company hired 10 persons on temporary basic as store assistants to take the inventory and record in computer. Since I am the only person in the group who has some previous knowledge of the computerized system, I am assigned the task of coding the materials. Since the store manager has high appreciation of my work, he recommended for a permanent job as computer data entry operator in his department. He completed the appointment order and took me to his boss, the financial control. To my misfortune I met Raouf in that office and there end my job in that company.

I already resigned from the work in the school and became jobless.

I paid KWD 5 for a bus pass for three month travel in bus No. 102 running between Kuwait City and Fahaheel. This is the longest bus route, but this is nearly two kilometer away from residence. Early morning, I will catch one of the buses in this route to hunt for a job. I knocked thousands of doors, nothing opened for me. Finally I abandoned the attempt when my bus pass expired.

5 of the 7 people who came from India with me joined a construction company building the Mubarak Al Kabeer Hospital as manual workers. I also joined them on daily wages basis and burnt my arms pulling the hot metal pipe lying in 50 degree centigrade open atmosphere. Fridays are holidays and I go their residence to spend the time instead of sitting at my home alone, thinking my problems.

One such Friday, when there was heavy rain with thunder, I noticed that one man was standing very close to the western side wall of their room fully wet. I called him to come inside the room instead of standing in the raining.

Because of his dark skin and long nose, everyone thought that he is not a Malayalee, hence others who know only Malayalam did not talk to him. One of them, Ayub offered a glass of tea and another Abdul Rahman bought a towel to wipe water from his body.

He asked me "where are you from?"
I answered "from India"
He enquired "from which state?
Listening my answer that we are from Kerala state, he started laughing and told in Malayalam 'I am from Mayyanad in Quilon district'
I talked 'then we are neighbors, we are from Varkala'
"My name is Antony, what are your names?' he told.
We told him our names.

We talked on several things especially my pitiable condition. He said he would try for a suitable job for me.

In the end he said "I am waiting for a man who went to the next flat. When he comes out, I will go with him back to my home in Fahaheel"

He moved near to the door when the rain stopped. One man in his early fifties came out of other flat with two heavy bags, having more height than length and breadth. One pickup van was waiting for them outside the gate.

That flat is notorious for bootlegs run by a Goan lady and her Malayalee paramour.

After two days when I was sleeping in my home, enjoying the relief from the horrible heat due to heavy rain outside, I was awakened by heavy knock in the window of my room. When I opened the window I saw Antony and Ayub stand outside in heavy rain. I immediately opened the outside door and let them inside.

Antony told me "There is a vacancy suitable for you in my company. I tried to inform you through other source, but could not find any one. So, I took a pickup van and came here. I took Ayub on my way because I do not your residence."

I went with him on the same pick van for which Antony paid KWD 5, a big amount at that time.

Thus I got a suitable job in an American construction company, Foster wheeler Energy Corporation. This company is constructing oil refineries for Kuwait National Petroleum Company in the most toxic areas of Kuwait. The work starts at 5'O clock in the morning and ends at 8 in the night, 15 hours daily with an extra payment of 7 over time hours. I have to get in the company bus at 3:30 AM to reach there on time. Fridays I work only 8 hours up to 1 PM to get 12 hours payments. A good earning helped to meet the marriage expense of my youngest sister.

One Friday evening my colleague Saad Taha, an Iraqi accounts clerk invited me for an entertainment function where he was also singing and I went with him, enjoyed my whole evening, the first time in Kuwait I laugh after reaching Kuwait. That day my beloved father died, but I came to know that after two days only. I have no telephone contact number and the fastest method of communication to me is telegraph. The telegraph sent by my family to inform the departure of my father from the earth is lying in the post box while I am entertaining with my friends.

When I informed the demise of my father to immediate boss, he put two options to me. He said 'the company will complete the work within two months. If you want to go home now, you have two choices. First one, you go for 10 days emergency leave and come back, and continue to the work another one month maximum. Second thing is that I can terminate you and give your full termination benefits. You can go home and stay there whatever days you wish.

I chose the second option and left that company.

I prepared to travel to India and went to the sponsor to get my passport, he ask me to bring Asmabi to get the passport. Asmabi also left the work in his house after completing the visa formalities of mine.

I approached Asmabi for the passport. First she refused to come with me but when I offered KWD 50 to her she came with me.

Catching a taxi, myself, Asmabi and her paramour Haneefa went to the house of the sponsor. She told me and Haneefa to wait outside the gate and she went alone inside. The sponsor was not in the house at that time, so we wait there for nearly one hour.

When he returned he was angry to see myself and Haneefa standing in front of his house. Haneefa and Asmabi went to him to talk about my passport, which made him more irritated. He took his head turban rope and start beating Asmabi and Haneefa. I run away from the scene frightened and stand in the bus stand waiting for them. After ten minutes they came out searching for me and informed me that he will not give my passport.

I tried to find a solution through Indian Embassy, but Sali, a relative of Asmabi who has grudge to her, told me that he would talk to sponsor and solve the problem for KWD 50 as his benefit. I agreed that and we both met the sponsor. The sponsor and his son who knows English talk to us inside their building compound. His son explained to me "she told us that you are her nephew and you are an orphan living on her mercy. You will work for us"

Sali said to them "All she said are untrue. This boy is the son of a high officer in India and he is highly educated. Here he was working as a school teacher and now as accountant in an American Company."

The son asked me "What is your qualification?"

I said "Master of Science"

He told to his father "he is very much educated. It is a sin to keep him here"

The father agreed to give my passport, but the residence permit was expired by this time.
The father said "I will cancel your residence permit and return your passport. You go back to India"

Sali intervened and requested him to renew the residence permit for a payment. That man demanded KWD 300 for one year residence permit, because he paid the visa free. After a hard bargain, we reached an agreement for renewal of the residence permit for one year for KWD 200.

He asked me to meet him two days after with KWD 200.

Now, more than two months has passed since the death of my father, Also my purse became empty after payment of KWD 50 to Sali and KWD 200 to the sponsor.

My old company has completed their project and left Kuwait. One of colleague, Ali Yousef Kunju joined a Japanese company, I H I Middle East in their construction site of a power plant for the Kuwait government. One day he informed me that there is a vacancy in the accounts department of that company and if I am interested meet him the next day. I joined this company and worked there until the completion of that project.

There I met an Engineer, Nazrulla, who is only a native of our town in India but also a close friend of my cousin, Dr. Abdul Hadi, now a professor of the University of Kerala.
He is staying with the family of Rafeeq and thus I acquainted with him also. Later I shifted my residence to there, when Nazrulla changed his residence when his wife and children joined him.

One day, Rafeeq arranged a reception to two wealthy exporters from India, one of them is a relative of Rafeeq. They came here to promote their export business. Unaware of the facilitation I went that house with Nazrulla. As a coincident I met Koya an old classmate of the relative of Rafeeq. They body recognized me because my eldest brother Vaheed was also their classmate and they came to my house in India several times with my brother.

By this time, I am mentally recovered and my thought resorted to my old passion, research.

I tried a job in Kuwait University through the recommendation of Mr.Koya and run after it for eight months. By this time my residence permit expired and my purse became empty, which forced me to search a job.

Antony has joined a house hold item trader as an account and working for them for a very mean salary. When he got a better job in an Air ticket office, he asked me to work in the house hold shop until I find a suitable job.
He told me 'Misbah, to be frank I am keeping you and your passport as a pledge to him for the money I borrowed from him. I will return the money from my first salary in the new company and release you.'

Considering his assistances to get a job and on other occasions I agreed to him. Foods are not allowed inside the office of Foster wheeler. He will skip from the office around 12:30 PM every day and go to the nearest city and bring food for all of us and keep in the time office. We will go one by one there and eat, otherwise I could not continue there for 15 hours work.

He did as he promised and released me when he got his first salary.

One day, one of my friends, Mohamed Ali told me that there is a vacancy in his company and meet him the next day. He warned me that, I do not tell anyone that I came there for a job, if anyone asks me.

I met him the next day and he coordinated with an Iraqi man, who is migrating to Canada. My job application and the Iraqi's resignation letter are submitted jointly by Mohamed Ali to the Deputy General Manager of the company Mr.Fahad Misfer.

Thus, I joined Al Muzaini Exchange Company, the oldest and leading private financial company as a clerk in the International Division in the year 1980. Since it is a financial company dealing with plenty of cash, I am compelled to change my residence permit. The company gave me a new visa. To change the residence permit, I cancelled the old residence permit and went to Cyprus and returned with the new visa.

Cyprus is a place with a lot of vegetation and the air is filled with plenty of oxygen. Inhaling the fresh air after four years of sulphurous foul smell was a great medication to me and three days stay there enable me to recover my health to a great extend.

One day, Antony called me and asked a loan of KWD 100/—for deportation of an old and sick unemployed person. I asked him why he is helping others by borrowing money. He answered "the money is for needy, not to keep in the bank"
I asked him "Are you aware that you have two daughters. You have to save not only for their education but to pay their dowry"

He made a deep breath and said 'they have some gold ornaments. That is enough"

I did not argue with him, but I paid that KWD 100.

Three months after, one person came to me and gave me an envelope containing KWD 100, saying that Antony sent him to me. It was a time when he was planning to send his eldest daughter on marriage to a college lecturer.

I telephoned him and asked
"Uncle what have you done. I kept some money for you to conduct the marriage of your daughter"

He replied "If something happens to me today, you will lose your money. Fortunately you are the only creditor"
I told him "Do not talk about the death."

Next day, Ali Yousef Kunju called me and said "You know, Antony uncle died last night by heart attack and his body is taking to India today evening"

It was a shock for me since I remembered his talk last evening. We have a feeling that he is an atheist because he never goes to church and talk about religion. On the other hand he treated people of all community same and assisted all needy. Many people talk about him "he is a man who forget to live himself and lived for others except his family"

Ali Yousef Kunju explained "last night he had a heart attack and admitted in Adan Hospital. He died around 12 midnight"

He continued "His body is kept in the mortuary of Sulaibhikhat. It will be kept for public tomorrow around 2:30 PM"

Here, irrespective of the religion, all the dead body is moved the mortuary near to the grave yard. Friends and relative can have look there and can either bury here or take it to their native country.

I went to see his remains, but his brother, a high officer of Kuwait Airways arranged all required things and the body is flown to India by noon.

Few months passed eventless until the Iran Iraq war erupted in the year 1980. The cost of living shoot up like rocket and an insecure feeling grabbed all minds. Expatriate sent all their hard earned savings to their native places.

The crash of Souq al Manaq compounded the problem. The words "Souq Al Manaq" mean the market at Camel Sitting. This is a trade center for stocks and shares at an Air Conditioned Camel shed, parallel to the official Stock Exchange. The official stock Exchange is considered as a market for rich and influence people only. People purchased whatever shares available in the market at higher prices settling by post dated cheques and sold at profit taking again post dated cheques and that activities continued like a chain. Banks and financial institutions discounted these cheques and paid these, until all the cheques bounced back at the maturity. The total of such cheques is estimated to around US$ 94 billion which exceeded the total revenue of Kuwait in that year. It is the considered the highest collapse of a speculation.

People was enjoying fabulous life, enjoying extreme luxuries with the fallacious profit obtained in Stock market.

A total collapse of the system prompted government intervention and a lot of strict restrictions were imposed. Much felicitous life fell like farce.

Kuwait was siding Iraq in its war against Iran, that provoked the Shiite Communities of Kuwait and Iraq. They considered the war as an attempt to their religious right by destroying Iran ruled by Shiite Clergies.

It is estimated that Kuwait paid Iraq over seven billion U.S. Dollars in addition to all their arms and ammunitions.

In the year 1983, an extremist group of Shiite based in Iraq, has bombed the Kuwait passport office, petro chemical industries, two embassies and some important locations within 20 minutes in a day.

That day I was expecting visas for two of my brothers Vaheed and Himad and two for my cousins Elah and Kader and the agent was in Passport office to collect them, at the time of the bomb blast. He received the two for my cousins and was waiting for the rest when the incident took place.

One of my cousins Elah joined a good job and spent four years here and returned to India to rejoin his old occupation of Principal of a deaf and dumb school there.

Other person, Kader was a terrific experience for me, he not only default the money spent by me for his visa and ticket, but also he demanded money to me for all his needs. Although he also left the country after four year, he was a burden to me till his death.

My eldest brother, Vaheed was an engineer in a prestigious company in Dubai who fell suddenly ill. Doctors indicated that if he continues his liquor consumption, his heart and kidney will protest soon. He should stop the consumption of liquor immediately, which he tried in vain. So, he was wishing to migrate to a country where the liquor was not available. At that time, Kuwait and Saudi Arabia were two countries in the Middle East where the liquors are prohibited.

Being member of a very conservative Muslim family and grandson of the Chief of Muslim cleric of Odayam 'mahal' (area), sons of the most educated and respected person of that locality, people look at him as a bad boy who spoiled the ethic of the family. He became isolated in the house as well as in the society.

But, no one knew that he was trying hard in vain to abandon his habit. He hated himself.

This made me to take the decision to bring here in Kuwait to spend his remaining life with me.

There are several stories linking to his alcoholic habit, the most prominent one is an incident connecting him to a lady. He was in deep love with that lady, which he could not disclose to our family fearing that their marriage will be rejected because of the social and cultural background of the families. That lady married to another man and stayed in the building opposite to him in Dubai.

Another story is that he has loved a lady who is proposed to his younger brother. Hence, he kept his love as sacred and his lost love fumed on him and he pour liquors to put the fire out.

Whatever may be stories, I know he is a voracious reader and a great painter in addition to his excellence in his work as a Mechanical Engineer. He spent most of the days at work place and nights for reading and painting. He takes a peg, lay in the easy chair, reads or go to stand, fill it with good portraits.

Expecting the visa, he went to India and stay at Chennai, a city far away from our native place, just to hide his illness from other members of the family.

The younger brother, who has a reputed job in India, very near to his house, wants to come to Kuwait as treasure hunter. Many people are coming here and earn a lot and their luxurious life during the short vacation, incited him to go to Gulf. He does not understand that these luxuries are for a short period and he has to work for years to clear the indebtedness. Once his loan is cleared he will plan the next vacation. This is the conditions of majority of expatriates.

I lost the money paid to the agent for the visas, but the thing which worried me most is my eldest brother. I am keeping the great secret that he is sick from others, a promise I gave to him.

He waits six months for the visa and then return to Dubai. The most difficult thing in the life is to change the old habit; he continues his liquor, reading and painting. He must find out a source of income for his living, an engagement with full freedom and without external control.

With the small amount of money received from me and a loan from a friend, he purchased a small dormant business run by one of his acquaintance. He become over enthusiastic and finds some business, especially a contract for maintenance of an old small ship. It was a successful entrepreneurship which earned him income to settle his loan to his friend.

Moreover, it was a morale booster for him and gradually he concentrated in his work and reduced the liquor and other activities considerably. One he told me over the phone "Now I am free from my vice. In near future I will be a saint"

Soon he got another, which provides him with enough income for renovating his office and workshop. More employees were added to his workforce to enlarge the company to be a medium type of business.

Thereafter there was lull period and he was forced to idle for months. He started to take some austerity measures to reduce the expenses and demanded more money for survival.

He was very much depressed and spent most of the time at home. It is said 'old habit is the best friend who accompany still your death'. He finds his solace to liquor, books and paintings to spend his day.

In the year 1984, our mother died and we both went to our native place for her funeral. We both met there after a gap of 12 years and discussed several family matters.

He persuaded me to marry to my cousin, whom he was much fond of, despite her father's great enmity towards him. I wondered why he acted like this. She is much younger than me and of the same age of our nieces.

I felt sorry for him; here is a desperate man, whose each heartbeat is filled with love and affection for all, even to the person who considers him as a foe.

He told me "He is retired; poor and cannot arrange a suitable marriage for his daughter"

Why this man is hated as a drunkard, especially by those who accepted many favors from him?

May be he is not married because he does not want destroy the future of a girl, due to his bad habits which he is trying in vain to get rid of.

Before my marriage to the same girl, he returned to his old business in Dubai.

To add his strait, he got a construction contract, which demands a great amount of investment. It was a much awaited project; hence his present financial problem did not prevent him from pursuing the contract.

I also arranged some money for him by taking loan from my employer and joining two chit funds.

I was member to two chit groups and since my journey to India was fixed suddenly and not pre planned I gave an authorization letter to a friend to bid the chit and send the funds to me India.

That person was unfaithful and he did not remit the funds to me after bidding at the highest margin and collecting amount from fund manager.

I already had a loan taken for the marriage expenses my youngest sister, which was an arranged marriage like the custom of our society. Actually it over burdened me and I struggled much to meet my both ends.
He completed the project with a very small profit, but the owner of the project, Mr. Abdullah Al Bukhasim insisted that he would retain 20% of the contract money for one year. He could not settle the debts to his suppliers fully.

He could not find a way to overcome this problem and most of the employees left the company since they were not paid for several months. I could not assist him, except occasional remittance of very small amounts for his living expenses.

He negotiated with several prospective buyers of the company in vain. He confined himself in his room, sipping liquor. All his friends deserted him and his creditors visited occasionally to abuse him.

He expressed his desire again to come to Kuwait to me. To save his life I had no alternative but to try for a visa for him.

Another unfortunate incident stopped the process; he had to wait there for an indefinite time.

In the year 1985, two suicidal bombers, filled their two vehicles with gas cylinders and hit the motorcade of the Amir of Kuwait in front of the entrance of the Sief Palace. Two patriotic young body guards stopped them and burst into pieces. The Amir escaped with minor injuries.

The intensity of the blast was such a high level to think that the hundreds of building in that area collapsed in an earth quake of high degree. The several glass windows were broken and spread over the floor in hundreds of pieces. Was the building shaking or was I shivering?

There was stand still in Kuwait and all activities were stopped. Police checked each and every house to find any culprit and unauthorized residents in Kuwait.

Many people are questioned and vehicles are stopped for checking the civil identity cards. People are forced to start their journey one or two hours earlier to reach their destination on time.

Finally I got the visa for my brother in the second half of year 1987. It was a mental booster for him and he started the preparation to pack up from Dubai. He and the sponsor of the company negotiated with Mr. Abdullah Al Bukhasim for the retained funds. And the part of the amount was recovered and the rest will be paid to the sponsor.

He reached an agreement with one of his old class mates in the Engineering College, Mr.Radhakrishnan Nair, to sell his company.

With the part payments received from Mr. Abdullah and Radhakrishnan, he cleared his outstanding debts to be free to fly to Mumbai for visa formalities.

Again tragedy struck him, his passport was missing. He checked everywhere but could not trace it. He believes that the passport is held by the sponsor, who does not want to give him because he gets benefits if Vaheed stays there.

The only solution was to apply for a new passport which would take one month. Another one week was taken to stamp the exit permit in the passport from UAE government.

Then, he sent the visa back to me to change the passport number from the old to new in the visa.

He traveled to Mumbai with Mr.Radhakrishnan Nair, who promised to pay him the balance of the purchase amount of the business in Mumbai. He landed Mumbai with an empty valet, not even the money required to telephone me from there.

Unable to pay for a hotel, he requested the assistance of one of his old employees, who offered to him a corner of his single bed room apartment to keep his belongings and sleep.

He was much ashamed and felt as if he is a beggar, wandered in the street of Mumbai, lied that he had his food from outside. How long can he starve?

Third day, he managed to sell some old stuff to meet his daily expenses. He took his first solid food in three days from a nearby restaurant and caught a train to Thane, a township 150 kilo meters away from his residence, to meet Mr.Radhakrishnan Nair.

It was on 27th December 1987 and the same day night, I received a telephone call from Nair's Hospital, a well known institution in Mumbai that he was admitted in the incentive care unit and the chance of his survival was very remote. They got my telephone number from his pocket diary and they called other numbers in the diary, every one told them to contact me.

I immediately called to my home in India and asked my other brothers to go to Mumbai immediately. They sent two of my relatives, Kader and Rashif with a good sum of money to give the best treatment to him.

At the same time, I requested to one of my old classmates, Shahid who is running a travel agency in Mumbai for assistance. I wire transferred a good some of money to him to meet the initial expenses and hand over the remaining to my two relatives who might reach there next day morning.

Shahid sent two of his employees to the hospital and arranged hotel accommodation for my relatives.

Kader and Rashif went directly to the hotel from the airport and rest there till evening. They were planning how to enjoy with the large amount of money brought for the treatment of my brother. That day evening, they went to the travel agency office and enquired the condition to the persons who visit the hospital.

Rashif asked them "Can you spend your time in the hospital until he dies? You telephone me when that happens"

Kader said to one of them "Dinesh, you do it, you will be paid well".

They went back to the hotel, enjoyed with liquor and prostitutes and slept, while one man was laying in the hospital waiting for someone to pay for the medicine and hospital fees for an emergency surgery. Since the money not reached, he was neglected.

29th Dec. 1987, I reached Mumbai Airport in the early morning plane and tried to get out from there through green channel because I had nothing valuable for paying the custom duty. The customs officer questioned me and asked me to wait until they clear the other passengers.

I told him "Sir, my brother is admitted in the Nair's Hospital in a critical condition, I want to reach there as early as possible"

The officer said "In Mumbai we hear hundreds of such stories, you wait"

I replied "I can open my bag and show you, there is nothing except two saris and 2 baby dresses"

He responded: "You wait; otherwise you pay Rs 5000 to customs"

I answered "I have only Rs.2000 cash and rest is bank draft. I want to go to Dadar"

He smiled and put his hand on my shoulder "Give me Rs. 1500 and rest is enough for you to reach Dadar"

I paid him, took my bag and came out of the Airport.

To my astonishment, no one was in the Airport to receive me. I had a faint memory of the travel agency office, which processed my visa formality when I first traveled to Kuwait. I took a taxi and reached the Travel Agency office.

I met the gentlemen, Kader and Rashif in that office, intoxicated spelling out something which I cannot grasp. We went to the hospital with one Dinesh. On the way, Dinesh talked to me the services rendered by him to my brother and his expectation of good remuneration.

As soon as I entered the hospital, one Malayalee Nurse, Elizabeth told me "You are very late. He should have been saved if you reached yesterday"

I thought he was dead and started sobbing.

I asked her "When it happen"

She did not answer me, but she guides me alone to the ICU where he is laying waiting his end. Others were standing outside waiting for the permission because only one person was allowed at a time.

His eyes was flowing, I guessed that he wanted to say something to me. I put his hands on his hand and listened to hear from him. Nothing happened, he could not speak.

I came out from ICU and stayed outside waiting for Elizabeth. Actually she was behind me.

She told me "We all prayed yesterday to hear from you. An expensive surgery was arranged for his legs. No one came"

After a pause, she continued "they amputated both his legs to save his life. If I have money I would have paid them that eleven thousand."

"When he came to know that he had no legs, he begged the doctor for a mercy killing" she uttered with sorrow.

She was not stopping
"He did not eat or drink anything since then"
"I called you day before yesterday. Why do not you come on the same day or next day? Here everything is money. Without money life has no value, especially in hospital"

Dinesh who was hearing the conversation said "myself came here yesterday with my friend. I enquired in the reception"

She became angry "did you come inside to see the patient? If I saw you I would tell you about the operation"

I met the doctor. Pretending that he was very busy, he told me "you are very late. Now the chance for his survival is very remote."

"What can he do without leg? Begging?"

I was much saddened by his words.

Here lays a great philanthropist, scholar, painter and entrepreneur who do not receive any recognition from the society.

The question still unanswered "Is it an accident, suicidal attempt, murder for theft or murder attempt by quotation group."

CHAPTER 4

M Y MIND STILL perturbed by the thought of my brother laying in the death bed and I stood outside helpless.

Kader and Rashif joined us in the evening, as evening outings from the hotel where they spend the times since morning.

Dinesh was persuading me to go back to the hotel. He was hungry; no food was consumed since he joined me in the morning. I was starving because that man is my brother, but why should he?

We left the hospital and he took us to one of the expensive restaurants for the supper.

My belongings were left in the Travel office, which was closed since one hour. Dinesh came with us and at the hotel gate he took from me Rs. 500 for the taxi fare and went on the same taxi. I know the maximum taxi fare would be Rs.100 but I paid in consideration of the time he spent with me since the morning.

In the corridor of the hotel, their new friend, a local pimp was waiting. They occupied two adjacent rooms in the 2nd floor, while my room is in corner of the third floor. There is no spare dress with me, so I removed my shirt and shoes and fell on the bed.

Next day morning, I woke up early as usual, completed the routine work and came out of the room around 7'O clock.

First I knocked the door of Rashif, he was still fast asleep and did not respond. Then I went to Kader, who was also sleeping. After two minutes he opened the door and I entered.

An half finished bottle of whisky stood as a minar over the wardrobe and a bunch of flowers usual worn by Indian prostitutes were lying in his bed crushed.

There was a folding chair in that room and I sat on it.

Lying in the bed, he said' "Why we go early. Visitors time starts at 9 only"

I told "We must reach there before that"

After some time I awaked Rashif also and entered inside the room. It looked like a battle ground, a bottle of empty Rum was lying on the ground and another bottle was kept on the table. There were several women's utilities which caused me to think that more than one lady were in that room last night.

He also complained that I wake them early and stayed in the bed some more time.

They are ready by 9:30, but Rashif wants to meet Shahid first before going to the hospital.

I told 'we will meet him today afternoon'

He replied 'I do not collect the amount you remitted to his name so far. We will collect it now. I have only little money'.

I asked him 'How much you brought from home'

He said 'only 70000'

'That is a good sum; you spent it in three days' I said "so far nothing is spent for the treatment. Now we need more money'

He did not answer me.

I continued 'We will collect the funds this evening, first we will go to hospital"

Rashif said 'I have to meet him for another issue'

I enquired 'What is it?"

He again kept quite.

'Ok we will go to his office, but spend only five minutes there' I said.

When I reached the office there were more than 50 people waiting for Shahid, most of them from my native place.

Each of them paid Rs.50,000 for getting a visa to Bahrain before two months by borrowing or selling all their valuable possession or pledging their home in the Banks.
Shahid arranged an accommodation for these fifty plus persons, which was suitable to keep maximum ten people. They were getting one time food from Shahid and they collectively cook something, most of the days rice broth for one more time. Seeing their pathetic conditions some persons donate small amount to them.

Dinesh was the only staff present in the office.
He said 'Shahid sir will be late. These people are also waiting for him. He has gone to collect their visas'.

I knew what he was not saying the truth, most probably Shahid will not come to the office.

Dinesh told me "Sir, if you go for breakfast, take these people also, they don't eat anything since yesterday noon."

That made me to go to the restaurant with these miserable persons, and Dinesh asked them to pray to God Almighty for my brother.

From the restaurant, myself and Kader proceeded to the hospital while Rashif stayed back to meet Shahid.

On the way to hospital, Kader initiated the talk about their spending.

As a complaint he said "I am your first cousin, he is the son of your second cousin. Still your brothers handed the money to him. In the first day alone he spent more than Rs.30000 for party, liquor and girls"

I was angry 'you are elder than him and you are one generation up. Why do not you stop him? Why don't meet brother for whom you came to Mumbai?'

I knew Kader a cheap womanizer who fell to the provocation of the younger man.

He replied 'We met a friend of Rashif at the travel office and they went together to the bar. I wait them for hours and then I went to the place where he is sitting"

He continued 'His friend left only yesterday morning'

'What is the issue with Shahid for him' I asked 'is it for his visa'

'That I don't know. Shahid is a cheat, he cannot do it' he said.

I don't want to continue that talk. I know Kader is trying to tell me that he is innocent but I know there are grave mistake from him also. If they have gone to hospital as soon as they reached Mumbai, my brother's life will be saved.

Rs.70000 is equivalent to Kuwait dinars 2000 which is my four month salary. They spent it in two days for liquor and women instead of saving the valuable life of my brother.

Kader told me "Tell Shahid not to hand over the money to Rashif"

We went to a telephone booth near to the hospital and called Shahid. He told me that he did not collect the money so far from the bank and promised to pay me the full amount tomorrow

I told him 'the money with me is not enough to meet the hospital expenses and take him to my home'

He replied 'don't worry, I will arrange'

We went directly to the ICU and stayed in front of the door. When one nurse came out, I enquired to her the condition of my brother

She said 'he is sinking; it will be over at any time. So wait outside' Around 2:30 PM. Rashif and Dinesh joined us. Rashif was mood off because he did not receive money from Shahid. They wanted to take lunch and I joined them.

Kader is chain smoker; hence they stayed outside of the hospital building while I sat alone in front of the ICU. They are least bothered about the condition of my brother.

They came to me and Kader said "Now the time is 10:30. If we delay we do not get any food. Let us go now and come tomorrow early morning'

I gave my hotel telephone number and room number to the hospital reception and asked them to call me if anything happen.

'Ok you will be informed when he dies'

After the supper, we went to the hotel. I told them "tomorrow early morning I will go to hospital. They can come at any time'

Next day is the last day of the year 31st December 1987, may be the last day of a life in this world.

I got ready at 7:30 AM to go to the hospital after a sleepless night. Since the last day's experience was in my mind, I did not want to awake Kader and Rashif to avoid any delay. I opened the door, to my astonishment I saw both were standing in front of my room fully dressed.

We had our breakfast and reached the hospital around 8:45 AM. Still there is 10 to 15 minutes to allow visitors inside the hospital.

Elizabeth, who was on weekly holiday yesterday, greeted us with faint smile. She was waiting for me to inform that Doctors abandoned the case of Vaheed and he was breathing his last.

I told to my relatives "She is the only merciful person I met in this city"

Rashif said "May be for money"

I replied 'Don't think that way'

Later Kader told me that Rashif approached her for sex and she scolded him saying "Do you think that everyone is like the ladies who come with you. You come to Mumbai to enjoy while your relative is dying. If you pay the money for the surgery he would have saved"

Is he the merciless or addict of liquor and ladies?

Time passed very slowly and day was very lengthy.

After 10:30 PM no visitor was allowed inside the hospital, hence we came out to stand in the staircase from where we could see an open play ground. The weather was very cold.

Makeshift stalls and platforms were seen in the nearby play ground for the New Year celebration.

Western music was flowing through loud speakers and people started gathering there.

Around 11:30 PM Rashif said 'I am chilled. I will come after ½ hour"
Kader said 'I am also coming with you'

They did not tell me where they were going, but I could guess that they went for the New Year celebration.

In the intoxication, they were dancing for welcoming a prosperous new year. Sharp 12 there were firework and shouting by hundreds of people.

As same moment, Elizabeth came outside and informed me in a very painful voice "He is dead."

She did not wait to see my agony

Nobody is nearby to share my sorrow, and I had no method to contact my relatives.

I went to the nearby telephone booth, it was closed. I came back to the hospital; I tipped the gate keeper and told him my requirement. He took me inside and gave me a phone.
I tried to call the residence of Shahid, there was no response, May be he also in the New Year party.

I sat on the staircase, put my head over my knees and wept still the dawn.

In the morning, Elizabeth came to me and said "My duty is over. If you need any assistance, I can stay here".

I said thanks to her and took a bill of Rs.1000 and offered her.

She said "why you think this way, I never expected anything. He is a nice man. He talked to me several things when he gained his consciousness after the first surgery"

I said "sorry to hurt you"

She helped me a lot and continued her assistance until we took his body for embalming

Since it was an unnatural death, police came there for investigation, Rashif attend their queries. He told them Vaheed committed suicide and he had suicidal tendency for a long time. He signed their documents for winding up the investigation.

He repeated the same to my relatives at home; they still believe that it is a suicide.

What actually happened? Was it a suicide? Why cannot it be an accident, robbery or killing by hired murderers? Among these four options, suicide has the least chance.

Shahid took that as a good business opportunity, he arranges the ambulance, religious ceremonies, embalming of death body and Air tickets.

Vaheed's employee, who provided shelter to him agreed to deliver the belongings of Vaheed at the Airport, when we reach there. He did not come there and we telephoned him, which were not answered.

At the airport Shahid told me "This is not the proper time to talk about money. I will come there next week. We can settle it there."

He continued "I will collect the belongings of Vaheed and bring with me"

We reached Trivandrum airport around 11:30. One politician who slipped down in his hotel toilet in Mumbai was traveling on the same plane from Mumbai. Few of his sycophants gathered in the airport to receive him they blocked the main door of the Airport and shouted slogan, which delayed us nearly one hour.

Ambulance was waiting for us and he reached home within the next 20 minutes.

We reached home around 1 PM. His body was taken for burial after giving chances to our friends and relatives for a last view of him.

When everyone left after the funeral, one relative approached me and asked "How much savings Vaheed has?"

I am perplexed but replied "to my knowledge nothing'

He said 'I have little education but my savings are Crores, What kind of Engineer is he?'
I kept quite remember the assistance given by Vaheed to the direct brothers and sisters and other close relatives of this man.

I noticed that this man is trying to talk to me immediately after we reach home, but never expected that he is attempting to ask me this stupid question. He is working in an off shore oil company, hence he is get a high salary. He always offers assistance to others to get their appreciation, but never helped any one.

I still have three week vacation, but every five minutes I receive call from my office in Kuwait to take my opinion and solution for various issues. I am really fed up with this repeated call for even trivial issues, with no consideration of my mental conditions. Every night the General Manager of my company will call me to condolence, but the conversation ends with business issues.

As promised Shahid came to his home and called me after one week. We agreed to meet at well known restaurant. I took Rashif also with me because he was the person who dealt with Shahid.

Shahid billed more than five times of the charges of other agencies for each service and Rs.20, 000 for his employees for their "help" in the hospital. He took the advantage that the mourners of loss of a close relative would not think the financial matters.

Life is more precious than money, I kept quite.

Shahid and Rashif had consumed liquor from that hotel and talked several things in the tipsy mood. I distracted myself in their conversation which was mainly on the difference of various brands of liquors. But, I stretched my ears when I heard the world "Kidney" and money, but they again reverted to their old topic.

I remember the warning of the nurse Elizebeth of Nair's hospital "his Kidney is the problem".

I thought his kidney had problem and said "I will try to find out some donor of kidney for him"

She replied to me "I do not mean that". She hurriedly entered the ICU.

That day I asked Shahid to help me to find out a donor of Kidney for my brother, but he laughed as if I said a joke. I said "I said I am serious, if I can save his life I am ready to spend any amount."

He laughed again "without legs,? What is the use?"
After a pause he asked me "looking for a donor or some one to buy it from you?"

I replied "I want to save his life, he is an engineers and he can earn his bread sitting on a chair. I know no one in this city that is why I ask your help"

He responded "you have to pay two three lakhs for it"

"Try, I will manage" I said.

He was looking to Rashif all this time and I saw that Rashif is staring to me and Shahid when we finish our conversation.

Next day, I told Elezebeth that I am searching a donor for the kidney, but she replied "you are mistaken".

Then Rashif came forth hurriedly and asked her what Vaheed ate last night. She walked inside the ICU without answering him.

I hate the way they behaved in Mumbai and now I am suspicious that Shahid and Rashif have made an attempt to sell his kidneys. I still do not know whether they or any others have sold his remains.

I was thinking to make a visit to Mumbai notorious for criminal activities and make an enquiry.

Iran Iraq war ended in the year 1988 only because both countries were tired and not only their whole national wealth was spent and all their arm and ammunitions were exhausted.

When the clouds of war had rained out, I brought my wife in the December of that year.
She became pregnant here and went back to India in June 1990.

CHAPTER 5

U SUALLY MORNING IS most hectic time in a day for us, awaking early, toileting, busying to office. Today nothing to do, even the television is stopped.

After some time Mathew and family joined us. After a short discussion on the present condition our talk slipped to other issues, like Indian politics, marriage of Rafeeq's nieces, the newly built house of a friend Alex.

Every mind is relaxed and all decided to move with the wind.

Annama said "God will decide our future"

She continued "let me cook some food. Little rice and one curry. Only a few materials left."

She left with her twin daughters leaving Mathew there.

After they left, Mathew told "the girls were hysterical last night. We tried hard to pacify them. We knelt down and prayed still 3'O clock this morning"

Rafeeq said 'We talked in front of them, that was a mistake'

He did not forget to add "my son is trilled. He wants to go out to see the things, I stopped"

Rukkiya cooked some food and placed in the dining table. Seeing that Mathew left the flat saying we will meet again in the evening.

I went to balcony to watch the street, it is empty. The trailer is still parked in front of the commercial center.

I am anxious to know what happened yesterday. I telephoned a friend, he was also unaware of the things.

I called my family in India to know the condition of my wife. Her condition became better. They decided to keep her there till her delivery.

I asked my brother "Have you got any news about Kuwait. What the medias saying'

He explained to me "Iraq occupied Kuwait. Amir is safe in Saudi Arabia. His brother died to save his life. America told Iraq to withdraw their military immediately from Kuwait'

"what is your condition", he asked me

I said 'So far no problem. But we are not getting news"

He advised, "don't go out. Keep inside until picture is clear, Try to come here as early as possible"

I told this information in our next union to all, all were agonized.

There was no events worth mentioning on that day.

Time is crawling like a snail, to escape from boredom I took a book on banking practice to read. My mind was wandering and could not complete even a single page of it. I closed the book and sat idle keeping the book on my lap.

I became scared to sit alone, I lay in the bed closing both eyes and covered the body from head to foot with the blanket.

As usual, next day I woke up early morning for the morning prayer. After the prayer I peeped outside through the window.

I saw, the driver of the trailer was getting down from the driver's seat, he was sleeping inside the trailer that night.

He lit a cigarette and sat on the parapet of the commercial centre.

I opened the door to the balcony and stood in the balcony. No one in the street, no man no vehicle.

Around 9'O clock a few people came out of their residence and gathered in the street. Taking this as an opportunity, the driver of the trailer lit a match stick and put over the goods packed on it.

When it started burning like a wick of candle, the driver started shouting :Fire Fire".

He saw that people were running toward his trailer he claimed the top the it and cut the rope fastening the goods to it.

People took the falling cartons over their shoulders to their houses. More and more people came there and the whole trailer was unloaded in a few minutes and driver took his trailers and left that place.

That was the beginning.

After two three hours four or five men of middle ages appeared in front of the commercial centre with long iron rods and hammers. One of them was Fateh, a Palestinian residing in the fourth floor of our building and working for Kuwait Oil Company as a buyer.

They broke the doors of shops and looted. More people joined them and the whole shops were emptied

Two Iraqi military trucks came there. Some were scared and left, while others stayed with them helping them to load the things in their truck. The army took whatever they could.

Several more truck came and army loaded the good while civilians were looting. The army and civilians were coordinating things and no one feared the army men.

My fear is diminished now. I dressed up and got out of my residence. I stood in front of my residential building watching the scene. Arab expatriates initiated the looting, Iraq Military took over it and Asian also started to join them.

Shiite Muslims are the prominent business community in Kuwait followed by Bohra Muslims from India. Most of the Shiite Muslims are citizens of Iran and rest Kuwaitis.

My heart sunk seeing that unpleasant situation and I returned to my flat. After a while, there was a telephone call from the Financial Controller of my company, Mr.Ramzi.

He asked, "Misbah, do you know the condition of our offices"
I replied "So far no news. I will go there and check it. I will call you back"
He said "I am waiting your call"
I asked him "Do you know anything about Muzaini family"
He replied," All except one car crossed the Saudi boarder. Iraqis covered the border. If they see any Kuwaitis they will kill them"
I enquired "who are in that car"

He answered "Abdel, his wife and children and one of his brothers. Now they are hiding. I arranged it. Don't tell anyone"

I walked to my office through the main road which is empty. In the sides of the road some people were standing.

The office is intact. All shops in that area were closed. I was little scared because I could not see any human beings in that locality.

On my way back to home, I thought to go to Murgab branch also. So I deviated my route through the heritage market and crossed the road. When I reached the open ground behind Kuwait Finance House building I saw a man laying in the ground in the hot sun, dead or alive. I quickened my step and crossed the bus station. No bus was there in the bus station, but few people were there. To my astonishment, I saw one very small shop selling fancy items opened, who was going to shop at this time.

All shops in Murgab area were safe. May be the looters will come this area after exhausting the very big business centers.

On my way back to home, I passed through the side of the commercial area, where people were gathered for taking as much as they could. Only the textile centers are attacked so far.

When I reached home, I telephone Mr.Ramzy to inform the condition. He asked me to update every morning and evening and also to go to Fahed Al Salem street branch.

"Any other news" I enquired.

He responded "I met Abdel yesterday, arranged food items for them. He asked me to contact you twice a day and inform him the condition"

Now I get an assignment for 1 ½ hours in the morning and 1 ½ hours in the evening.

Next day, Fateh enter ed the lift carrying two stolen suite cases full of looted goods.

He asked me "why don't you join us. Now we earn 10 times more than our salaries"
He was depressed when I replied "I don't want others goods"

10 times salary? I know he is taking 3 to 5 times daily goods to his flat. I am sure it is already filled with loots. As a buyer for an oil company, he might have collected very high amount as commission from the shop owners. Their usual practice is that they will collect the unwritten customer copy from the shop and write the amount what they like.

Recently he purchased a BMW car in addition to his Benz car. Before two months he bought for his son a motor bike worth more than a motor car on which his eldest son Sameer were flying through the road with a gigantic sound and became an hero amongst children of his age.

When I was returning from evening visit of our company branches, I saw Fateh and his family walking through the street cursing loudly the Iraqis. I asked him the reason.

I enquired the reason to him. He replied "Iraqi harami, himar stopped me and took my car"
He continued "it is a new car worth Kuwait dinars fifteen thousand"

I tried hard to hide the smile blossoming on my lips because he was the person who started the looting. God is great.

The very next day I woke up hearing a big noise in the ground floor of our building. I went down to find the reason. All the expensive cars parked behind the building were stolen. Fatah was yelling and shouting because his Benz car also was stolen.

The man coordinating with Iraqis got the double blow and the third one happened after two days. Young Iraqi soldiers put an eye on the motor bike and tried to break the chain fastening it with the pillar of the building. His son first begged to them to leave it there saying that their two cars were lost. Who cares? They asked him to bring the key of the bike and the chain. When he refused they hit with the butt of riffle, and took him to flat to get the keys.

In that flat they found several fancy things, some looted good and other purchased by his father, the army men took some of them.

That is a three bed room flat rented by the father in law of Fateh, Yasin when the building was completed at a nominal rent of KWD 25 and recently increased to 40 while other flats having similar facilities were rented at minimum KWD 200/— In that flat 3 sons and 2 daughters were residing with their families. The total inmate including women and children in that building were not less than 30. How they stay there? They were spending plenty for luxuries, but spending most of the times in the corridors and staircases, disturbing the other residents of that floor.

After my usual round, I tried to call Mr.Ramzy as usual, but he advised me "Do not call me. I will contact you whenever I want"

Later I recognized that Mr.Abdel and family were staying in his flat and he shifted to his friends flat. From their three storied villa these Kuwaitis confined to a small flat to save themselves.

Next day morning I met a friend and chatted for some time. He was much worried of his brother who was staying at Khaitan, where mostly labors were staying.

He said "I have no news of him and there is no bus to take me there" "Why don't you try for taxi" I asked.
He told "Every one is afraid to drive the car in the street, Not only military but Iraqi civilians are also capturing the cars'

While standing the road side, we saw a car was coming from the east. We moved to the footpath, then the car stopped in front of us, The driver asked "Where do you want to go?"

My friend replied "Khaitan"
Pointing his fingers to the backseat he said, "First I will go to Salmiya to drop these friends and then we will go to Khaitan"

Since Salmiya is in the opposite side of Khaitan, we are not interested. But he said "If you stand here you will not get any vehicle"

My friend enquired "How much you want?"

"only six KD'" he replied.
I responded "Six KD to take one person to Khaitan ! Normally we pay ½ KD"
"Are you not coming with me.? Please come with me" my friend requested.
The driver of the car, an Arab of middle age with a short beard said "Before it is ½ KD. Now you have to pay KD 6 if you want to go to Khaitan. You will not get another car"

Now it is war time and there is no meaning to bargain with him.

I told my friend "It is very far. How can we return"
"God will show us a way" he said.

People from my native town are also staying there. Hence I decided to accompany him. I was little scared to go that distance.

All the passengers are Indians and we exchanged the news and discussed the future plan.
They are planning to go to Jordan through Iraq and catch a plane from there to Mumbai.
They told us that they heard some Indian traveled through Amman safely.

One of the two passengers to Salmiya told us "yesterday I saw a military truck carrying nearly 25 Kuwait ladies who were crying and yelling in loud"

Other man asked 'how Iraqi military treat them?'
There was silence for a few second.

After dropping the two gentlemen at Salmyia, we took two more people going to Fahaheel. They are from my home state, Kerala and are going to meet their friends for planning to exit from this country.

The car was a Toyota too old to attract any Iraqi and no Air condition was working. It was hot summer and I was very tired and had a nap. After sometime, I felt that some one was touching my face to awaken me. When I opened my lids, I was a soldier peeping through the car door window and his riffle was touching on my face. I was very much afraid and moved backwards. He asked the driver "only Indians, no Kuwaiti'
The driver said "only Indians".
"You" the soldier asked again. The driver said "Syrian"
He let us go.

It was in front of Bayan Palace which was fully surrounded by Iraqi Military. They check every vehicle for Kuwaitis and if any Kuwaiti is found, they take him.

After 15 minutes we reached Khaitan, we saw some soldiers there. My friend went to meet his brother and promised to meet me at the same place after ½ hour.

In the street, I met a friend of mine and asked him "Do they trouble you?"
He replied with a laugh "they are our friends, they are coming here to get some food, anything they eat"
He continued "Now Saqir is feeding the Iraqis".

Saqir was well know me and was the dish cleaner of hotel, where I used to eat. One person hired a whole building and furnished and accommodate four persons in each room and serve them food at a very low cost. This type of hotels is known as 'mess' and there are several such messes in Khaitan area. It looks like a hostel, but unauthorized by the Kuwait government, hence run secretly. They also sell food to outsiders and I was one of the regular customers of the mess in front of my rooms. In Khaitan all buildings were separated into rooms having one or two toilets in each floor.

The cook of that mess had an illicit affair with wife of the owner, which was one day caught by the husband. Hence he closed it. Saqir was the assistant for the cook at that time and some of the inmates and outside customers asked him to continue because they all can not shift to another place in a very short time.

I saw him asking a lender KWD 300 for a interest of 30 KD per month. The lender, Mr.Kuttan Nair is my neighbor in India and staying in the next room, along with three others. He told him to bring a guarantor for the money.

He requested several persons for the guaranty and at last he came to me. Since I was impressed with his confidence, I lent the money to him free of interest. With that KWD 300, he developed the business and expanded by buying the nearby grocery. He always treated me with high respect. Before I left that place to stay near to my office, he repaid his debt to me.

First I met Saqir who offered me a lunch, I said I already took food in the morning, so no need food now.

After talking to him for two minutes, I came out of his place, but he followed me.

Knowing that I work in a financial institution, he enquired "I have some money with me. How can I send it to India?"

I replied "There is no bank or exchange company now. You find some person who needs the money here and ready to pay in India. That is the only possibility now"

He asked me "Do you know any one?"

I said "If I find anyone I will inform you"

I saw Kuttan Nair standing in front of his house and I walked to him. He was very much gloomy because he lost all the money he lent at a very high interest.
He rejoiced "Before 6 months, I sent a big amount to buy a plot of land. I can live with that money if I reach home"

Shahuddin joined us and our casual talk turns to a serious discussion, how to go out of this country and reach India.

I told them the news heard from my co passengers in the taxi that the people were going to Jordan and from there to India.

We decided to go to Fahaheel to enquire it. I told them that my friend might be waiting for me in front of the restaurant and I would contact them within two days. They accompanied me to the restaurant and stayed with me until my friend came there.

We got a car going to "Maliya" which is nearly 2 kilo meter away from my residence. From there we walked to our residence.

Maliya is the first place where Iraqis started their killing in Kuwait. Hearing the noise outside, one India kitchen assistant came out of his work place, holding the kitchen knife used for cutting onion in his hand. Seeing that weapon, Iraqis fired at him killing that innocent man, the bread earner of more than 10 people in India.

When I reached my flat, Shaji said "Uncle your relatives just left here, They may be down"

He continued 'They wait here more than one hour. They give this letter to you".

I rushed to down and checked there, I could not find them.

I came back to the flat and opened the letter. It is written by Faizy, brother in law of my brother Himad and his maternal uncle,

Jalal. They also heard that people were going to India through Amman.

When I completed reading the letter, I heard the voice of Rukkiya "They came here in the lunch time. But I have no food to give them"

She said 'Today I cooked on rice brooth only, because there is only little rice left"

This is the first time since she reached Kuwait that she does not provide any food to a visitor in her house. You visit her house any time, you will be served with delicious food.

I decided to go to Fahaheel next day morning if any vehicle is available.

Around 9 in the morning, I stood in street to catch any vehicle going to Fahaheel. I could not get one although I wait in the hot sun for more than one hour., I returned to my flat.

On my way back I noticed that some one was entering the store room of the nearest grocery. I looked inside the store and found the grocery owner and he employee were taking one sack of rice from there.

I asked him "can you give me one sack and some curry items"
He replied "I have only rise and 'dal', I can give you if you take it secretly"
I agreed and paid KD 10 to him, he returned me KD 2 and his employee put the sack of rise and the gram inside the lift.

It was a 50 kilo bag of rice and I drag it to my flat from the lift. Mathew and family were also in my flat.

Seeing the food items, every one faces blossomed with happiness.

Mathew asked me "wherefrom you get this"

I narrated the incident and he asked me to get one for him. I promised him that I would try.

Rukiya said to Mathew "Do not worry, we will share this until it finishes"

Now I have two additional works, finding a vehicle to Fahaheel and searching for food.

One day a person offered me a lift to Fahaheel and I went with him. He dropped me in front of the residence of Faizy and promised me that he would take me back after one hour.

Faizy told me "If I have money I will take all of you to India"
I told him "I have nearly KD 150, that is not enough"
"If anybody give the money I can repay in India" he said.

Then I remembered the words of Saqir and told him "I know a person who can give us the money"

"I can give him a cheque drawn on Indian Overseas bank, take the money" he told.

"how much you want?" I asked.

He had eleven relatives here in addition to me. He told me to take equivalent of Rs.100,000.

Including him there are 12 persons, myself and my Khaitan friends are seven, Rafeeq, Mathew and their families.

Many Iraqis were providing transportations to Jordan border through Iraq in their buses. We decided to hire one having capacity to carry 42 people.

Then, our discussion turned to the situation of Kuwait.

Faizy said 'Many became rich by looting the Kuwaiti villas, even Karalites are doing the same"

Jalal continued "I know one Malayalee employee 7 or 8 persons to break the Kuwaiti villas and rob the things."

"What about the food" I enquired.
"We do not have rice, but we got some wheat flour when the nearest grocery opened" Jalal replied
Faizy continued "Last week I got some vegetables. One bedeoun was selling in the street".

Bedeoun are stateless people, neither Kuwaitis nor Iraqis. Now they are moving freely.
I asked Faizy "Which side of the street?"

"Go through Sanaya, you may find" he reply.

When the car driver came, I told them "You make the arrangement for the bus. I will arrange the money"

In the car, the driver said "I am afraid that there is not enough petrol in the car."

He asked a passerby where is the nearest Petrol pump.
He got the answer" No petrol pump is open here. If you go to Sanaya you can fill without paying"

So we decided to go Sanaya. In the street, we found a person selling vegetables. I purchased some potatoes and one cabbage and the driver bought only potatoes.

After filling the gas, we continued our journey to Kuwait city. When we reached, I asked him "what do you want"
He said "I went there for my work. So, I will be satisfied with anything you give me"

I gave him one 5 KD bill. He touched his eyes with the bill and thanked me.

It was a pleasant surprise for the family to see the potatoes and cabbage.

Now, Rukkya said "Today we all eat together. I will invite Mathew and family"

When she was cooking the food, she found that there is no salt. She took the salt kept in the dinning table to add taste to her curries.

She laughed and said "Tomorrow onwards every has B.P, No salty food"

It is the first time we all laughed after the Iraqi occupation.

After the food, I talked to them my plan to hire a bus and go to Jordan and from there to India by plane.

Rafeeq said "Khalil has dollars and he will arrange a safe journey"
"Rukkiya is diabetic and has other disease, she can not travel that much distance" he added.

Khalil was recently hired and brought to Kuwait from Dubai as the parts manager of a Japanese car company and he was a neighbor of Rafeeq.

Mathew said "there are 26 members from my family including women and children. All the six ladies are nurses. They will not get their passport at this time. So, we have to wait"
I enquired "Children, I can take them to your home"
Mathew said "Thanks, let them stay with us. We do not want to part with them at them time"

On 13th August 1990, I went to Khaitan to meet my friends and Saqir.

Kuttan Nair said "In my childhood I starved several days. Now I cannot be hungry for one hour. I am sick and diabetic. It is better we reach home early"

I asked him "You have no food"
He replied "I used to eat at Saqir's. Now a days Iraqi army is always there to eat and we are not getting food."
"you take the money from Saqir, we will share it in India" he continued.

I wait there for Shahuddin, who went for finding some food items.

Seeing me, Vasu another person from my native place came to us.

He said with a rejoice "Sir, I am trying to meet you"
I asked "for what"
He replied "I have plenty of Iraqi Dinar. I want to exchange it"
I enquired "Wherefrom you got the money"
He did not feel shame when he said "We are breaking the Kuwaiti houses and taking all valuables. Iraqis are coming with truck to buy it."
"We will keep the goods in a flat of Thomas sir, He will arrange the sale" he told.
I asked him "If Iraqi military see this, what will be your condition"
He answered "we have an agreement with a captain of Iraqi Army. We are paying him 1000 every day".

He said "I have invited Shahuddin and Kuttan annan to join our gangue"
Kuttan Nair "I am 56 now, still now I did not rob"
Shahuddin said "it is Haram. It is not good to steel others property"

Kuttan Nair is an atheist and Shahuddin is a very religious Muslim, both think that steeling the things is a bad habit.

"What Haram, it is money" Vasu said.

I asked him "We are going to India, are you coming with us"
He replied "Not at all, we may not come back"
Kuttan Nair responded "there are still several Kuwaiti villas to break"
Vasu said "Arabs are doing it for several day. We started only recently. Why can not we do what Arabs are doing"

Kuttan Nair asked "if you give us some Iraq Dinars, I will give the equivalent to your wife"
He said "I am ready, but I need a cheque from you as guarantee"
Kuttan Nair asked him "how you send the cheque to India"
He answered "my captain said that everything will be normal within 2 weeks"

I said "I will come to you if we need any money"

Shahuddin came empty handed. He was very tired because of the hunger and heat. Three days he did not take food.

"Why do not you take food from Saqir" I asked him.
He replied "I have no money. Now Saqir is serving food only to selected people and the army"
Vasu said "I can give you some food items. We take the food items from the Kuwaiti houses first".

Shahuddin said "I do not want stolen goods even if I die"

When Vasu left, I enquired Abu Salim, who does not go to India for more than 12 years. We went to his residence, where he is staying alone. His front door is locked from outside and we returned. Later we came to know that he is hiding his sponsor there and he open the door after convincing that no one is in the vicinity

From there we went to Saqir. He took us to the Kitchen and gave us foods.

He said: "I can not feed these people without money. One day I will run away from this place"

After a pause he continued "before there were plenty, now most of them went back to Iraq"

He gave a packet containing KWD 4000 and said "When I came to India, I will contact you. You pay me at the rate KWD 36 for Rs.1000."

I agreed.

He said again "If I cannot meet you within 6 months, you pay the money to my father. I will give you his address"

I asked him to give food to Kuttan Nair and Shahuddin until we travel to India.
He said "I will do whatever you ask me. I have that much obligation"

When we came out of the mess, I asked Kuttan Nair to keep the money.

He told "the Iraq soldiers are coming to our building for toilet use. One two army men slept in our bed locking the door from inside"

He continued "they are all teenagers of 18, 19 years old. These boys are very tired"

I gave them 20 KD from my pocket and said "I will come back when the bus is ready".

I was very scared to carry the currency with me; fortunately I got a car that can take to my house. I returned home.

When I reached home, Faizy and Jalal were there. This time Rukiya was very happy to serve them food.

I took them to my room and informed them the developments.

Faizy said, "Salim mama talked to a driver yesterday. He said we will take us on 20th of this month. Be prepaid"

'Can we find one earlier' I asked.

'We are also trying" he said.

We had to stay one more week. I told them "Only Kuttan Nair and Shahuddin agreed to come with us. Two colleague of Shahuddin may join us. These two families are not coming with us"

'I can arrange people. There are more than 200 people from Edava village staying in Fahaheel'.

'How can I contact you' I enquired.

He said "unfortunately the telephone is not working from today'

I checked the telephone of my flat, it is dead.

Jalal said "We will come here if any development".

I came down with them to see them off.
"It is very difficult to get a car from here" Faizy said.

We wait only 5 minutes, one car came and stopped in front of us.
Faizy said "Fahaheel".
The driver said "I will go first to Shuwaigh then to Fahaheel"
Faizy asked "How much you want"
He replied "three KD only"

They started their journey.

When I returned I saw the grocery owner standing in front of his store. I asked him 'Do you have any food items."

He replied 'if you want, I can give you one more sack of rice'

I remember the request of Mathew, so I said 'I need one, do you have any spices'
I got one sack of rice, two packet of salt, one packet each of chilly, coriander, and turmeric powers.

In front of the door of Mathew's flat I kept the rice bag and I called him. He was a heart patient, hence I kept it in his hall. He was extremely happy and asked me 'how much you paid'

I joked 'Saddam Hussain has paid it'.

I kept the packets of the spices on the dining table, changed my dresses and performed the noon prayer belated.

Refeeq told his wife to serve the food for me. I told them that I already had it from Khaitan.

Refeek want to sell his car and one Iraqi already made a bid.

He told me "if I do not sell it now, someone may take forcibly.'
He sold it and waited for Khalil to travel to India. Several airlines companies were operating from Iraq, but they all accept only US Dollars.

That day I slept earlier because I was very tired.

CHAPTER 6

WHILE GOING FOR the round up, I see a long queue in front of Al Ahli Bank of Kuwait, where I am holding an account with a balance more than KWD 4,000, a big sum.
I enquired to one person and he replied "they are paying KWD 300 for each account holder"

I asked him "What documents they need"
He replied "your bank card".

I went home and brought my card and stood in the queue. Hundreds of people poured there and queue became very lengthy.

Soldiers were controlling the crowed pointing the guns to them. The situation was calm and quiet until one military officer said "All people from Jahra area separate and stand in a different queue."

There may be some political motive for this. Jahra is the area bordering Iraq and they want to gain their loyalty to Iraq. The

Iraq military was doing many favors to this people, mostly stateless Bedouins.

Since the instruction was not clearly heard, there was a pandemonium and the shouting of the military men was not cared by the people.

There was nearly 10 persons in front me in the queue, hence I did not move from there.
One teenage soldier fired to the sky. The bullet hit on the projection in front the main gate of the bank and reflects toward the queue. It hit on the forehead of the person stood in front of me in the queue. He fell down and crawled in the floor, catch my leg with pain stopped his movement.

I stood numbed.

'Do not move" the order came from the military. Every one stood standstill.

That person was little higher than me, otherwise the bullet would have hit me. This is the second time I escape like a miracle.

My pant was dip in the pool of blood. Three Iraqi military police men came there with an ambulance and took his dead body. The police men called me and the man in front of the victim and took us inside the bank building. He asked us what had happened. The man with me was an Arab, he explained the things. Since the military man did not know English he asked me very little.

After questioning he asked us to collect the money and go home with a warning "keep your mouth shut"

My shoe and the bottom of my pant are already soaked in blood. It gave me uneasiness to walk because the shoe was sticking to the ground like a gum. I took some water from the water cooler in front of the next building and pour it over my shoes.

With the wet pant and shoes I reached the home. I removed the shoes at the door step and directly entered the toilet holding the shoes in my hand.

Rafeeq and Mathew and the ladies were sitting in the front hall and watching me. When I came out of the toilet, they enquired like a chorus "What happened".
I said "wait a minute, let me change the dress"

I removed the pant and wore another one and threw the old pant in a bucket that was filled soap water.

I sat in front of the eagerly waiting audience. I was weeping like a child when I narrated the incidence to them.

In the night Mathew and Annamma came to me with two persons to enquire that incident.
Their relative went to the bank and never returned and they were enquiring.

They asked me the shape and colour of the deceased person. Then they showed me photo and asked me "is this person?" I nodded my head in agreement.

After they left, Mathew told us story "His name is John, his wife is a nurse working in the same hospital of Annamma. Now she is in India and today delivered a baby girl."

What a tragedy?

I lay in the bed staring the roof of room, thinking what would have been my condition if that man was not taller than me. My wife was also in the advanced stage of pregnancy. She did not have enough education to get a white color job and no nearest relatives capable for supporting her. With two infant children what would be the condition of a very young lady without proper education.

I totally perturbed by the thought of his wife and new born baby.

I do not know how long I stayed like that.

I moved to the side of the bed, touching my body to the wall to give space for Mr.John. He lay in the bed beside me and started talking.

'She is still in labor room. I will call her after two hours'
"Where can I get the best sweet? There is one Sindhi shop in Murgab selling the best leddu. I will buy 2 boxes of Kitkat. What else."

"This is our first child. I must celebrate"
"Tomorrow I will sign the contract for my new flat. Everyone told me do not make any preparation before the delivery. They believe that something bad may happen if I do anything before that"

"I have to paint the flat; otherwise the smell will be there when the child comes"
"I want to appoint a servant. Wife got only 70 days leave, already 38 days have gone"
"Where can I get a lady to wash the baby? I know one who is taking KWD 100 each month"

"My friends told me Awladona is cheaper than UTG for children's dress. But UTG has better quality"

After a pass he continued "I would have been there. I did not get the leave" He heard his sigh.

I stretched my hand to take his hands, I am perplexed, and nothing is touching my hand. I lowered the hand to touch the bed.

It took some time to gain my consciousness and to cope with the fact that John was dead.

Next morning, Mathew came to me again with those two gentlemen to get more information. They did not know where was the remains of Mr. John kept.

Rukkiya served black tea to all, while sipping the tea one of those gentlemen talked about the John.

After hearing the news that his wife delivered a baby girl, John talked to him several things as an illusion without caring the present situation of Kuwait. To my amazement I heard the same thing what I listened last night.

There is no surprise or supernatural thing; it is the common thought of any new father. My mind has done that exercise because I will be a father very soon. My own thought is transferred to another person facing similar situation.

They decided to contact Indian Embassy for assistance and proceeded to there.

I did not regain my mood to prepare myself to go for the daily visit of our offices. I sat idle at home till the evening when I remembered about my passport which was required for my travel to India. No body from our group remembered that.

I met Kuttan Nair and Shahuddin, fortunately they held their passport. Kuttan Nair took it for renewal of the passport and Shahuddin was working with a sub contractor, hence he did not want to submit the passport to his company.

I went to the Head Office of our company and knocked the main door. The watchman came out. He was an Afghani man of middle age, he survived all these days with tea and biscuit kept in the kitchen for refreshment of the employee. One day I told him that there were some cashew nuts and bananas in my cable. He took it and ate, although the banana was a little decayed.

Today I carried about two kilo of rice with me, bundled in a packet. He was weeping when I gave to him and said "today is lucky day. In the morning Ramzi came and gave me two pocket of Kubboos"

He continued "I planned to lock the door and go to my friends. Now I got the food for survival"

I asked him "why Ramzi came here?"
He answered "he took all the passports and some cash from the counter"

So, the passport is with Ramzy and I have to meet him. That day evening I went to the residence of Ramzi. He gave me my passport and another eight Indian passports along with KWD 1200 for distribution among the Indians. I distributed the entire eight passports along with KWD 100 to each of them. Two hundred was kept with to deliver to two persons who held their passport before the invasion for residence renewal purposes. Before the money was handed over to me they left the country.

When I informed Ramzy, he said "Now no value for money, you can get nothing here for money. Keep it with you; you may need it on your journey".

I thought, now eight hundred KWD was with me which am enough for three person's journey, only five more people agreed to come with me, why should I take the KWD 4,000. Why cannot I return half of it to Saqir.?

Faizy and Jalal came to me the next day, I told them that. Faizy said "we are going for journey and routes are not clear. We do not know when we can reach home. There is no news from Jordan so far. Better keep the money"

They arranged a bus to carry 42 persons, 27 from our native place and remaining persons are booked by the bus driver himself. The bus will start from Fahaheel at sharp 6:30 PM on the 2nd day.

The driver was an Iraqi and he warned "on the way people would take all valuables from you, I have no responsibility"
"Better you sell your things here. If you want I am arrange buyers for a small commission"

Actually it is not a commission business, he buy himself at a price he wishes. Once it is placed in front of him for sales, it cannot be taken back.

I asked "How can we travel with such a person. Who knows where will he take us?"

"Once we enter his bus he will protect us. That is their nature" Faizy answered.
I said I am really scared. They said we had no alternative.

I enquired to them about their passports. Jalal held it because he was jobless at that time.
The Personnel Manager of Faizy's company was staying in the same building, hence he could collect it.

I accompanied them to Murgab from where a plenty of vehicles are going to Fahaheel. There we found a small crowd near the roundabout in from of the Municipality office. Some thing was hanging on a crane. We went closer to view it; it was a man in military uniform, some placard written in Arabic fixed to his body.

I asked one Arabi "What is written in that placard"
He answered "Warning for looters. That is not true. He is a Kuwaiti wrapped in Iraqi Military Uniform. I know him"

That scene was there for one week with foul smell and uncared warning. The looting continued and most of the shops were emptied.

From Murgab, I went to Khaitan to inform my companions there. Everyone wants to leave the country as early as possible.

We all agreed to reach Faizy's house before 4 PM on that day.

I am preparing for a journey.

I asked Rafeek and Mathew "Have you changed your mind? If so, I can arrange for you".

They said "We already arranged the things, but it will take some more time"

I have no neat dress.

I had only very few dresses and I used to give the one week dresses to the laundry, two persons from the laundry would come to flats, one will collect the dirty clothes and other will return the washed cloth on the day.

Unfortunately the dirty clothes were collected but the washed clothes not returned. Hence two set of clothes were left in the laundry.

Since there was scarcity of water, we are not washing the clothes at home. We wash ourselves once in three days in the hot summer.

I wore a plant which had an extra pocket under the belt where I can hide something valuable. I put some currencies and one new Rado wrist watch.
I divided the banknotes into four parts, some I kept in the pants pocket, some inside my socks and the rest inside my hand bag.

Around 1'O clock, Mathew and family came to see off me. Everyone was much worried about me when I said farewell to them.

When I reached Faizy's residence around 3.30 PM, only he was there.

He told me 'I do not think we can travel today'
I enquired "Why?"
He said "9 persons from our group do not want to come now. They want to stay here because there are only few Iraqi Army men are here. They expect they will also go soon."

"What you decide?" I asked.
"We are twelve now. We want to go. If life is saved we can do anything for our food' he replied.

'Then what is the problem" I enquired.
"We booked 27 seats in the bus" he answered. "Let ever one come"

Within ½ hour all the 18 persons expected by us came. We discussed the problem.

Salim, another uncle of Faizy said "let us go to the bus and talk to driver."
Another person, Kamal seconded him "If he is not agreeing we will pay the bus fare of all 27 people"

It is only walking distance to the bus. All, except Salim has only hand bag. Salim was carrying all his belonging in two suitcases and one hand bag. Others assisted him to bring the luggage to the bus.

I took the cash and gave everyone a portion to hide inside their dress or bag.

On the way we met two friends of Shahuddin, they also want to come but did not have money.

Shahuddin asked me "Can you give them KWD 300; they will give it back when we reach Mumbai"

I discussed it with Faizy and offered them the money. They asked us to wait 20 minutes to pack their things and reach the bus.

I said "Ok, we will wait there for you"

When we reached the bus, one person asked Kuttan Nair "have you booked the seats?'
Kuttan Nair said "yes. Why are you asking?"

"I tried to book for my family, but there is no seat available" he answered.

"How many are you?" Kuttan Nair asked again.

"We are eight, four elders and four children" he replied.

We agreed to give them the remaining seats to them. Kuttan Nair said "We have only 7 seats left. You have to adjust"

He answered 'two children are below 5 years, we will arrange'

I told him "Hardly 50 minutes left for the departure of the bus. Can u come before that?"

He left after answering "yesterday we made an attempt. Hence our goods are packed. We only want to dress"

The bus was parked there but driver was missing. His assistant said, he was sleeping inside the nearby mosque and would come on time.

The person who reserved the 7 seats was also not shown up so far. The time reached 6:30 PM, the arranged time for departure.

The passengers who booked directly with the driver are already reached there.

Salim said "if the driver asks us now to occupy the seat we will do it without waiting for them"

Kamal said "The driver is coming, let us waiting until others enter"

Jalal said, "See, they are arriving, the children are walking very slow"

Two persons run to them to carry their luggage to enable them to speed up. They were two men, two women and four children. One of the women is pregnant and very weak.

The driver asked us to enter first and occupy the back seats. We entered and gave a separate place for two families with us.

While entering the bus, the driver noticed the a card board box belonging to Salim and enquired "What is inside this"

Salim said "Micro oven"
'What is it, Open it" The driver asked him. He obeyed.
"Keep it with me, otherwise the people will take it when we reach Basra" He said taking the oven with him, which is kept under his seat.

After we entered, the driver counted our heads, he said including the children 27 persons.
Salim said, 'Do not count the small two children. They will adjust in one seat"

"Then there should be one more person from you group" he said.
"We booked only 27 seats and we are 24 grownups and 4 children" Salim said.
"No, you are 22 men and 2 ladies and children, count it" he insisted.
Jalal said "I saw Thaha getting down the bus with his bag" He went down to search for him, but returned alone.

Famy, a member of our group said "he came under my compulsion. He wants to stay here".

Then we told the driver, one man is not coming with us. He said he will charge us if he could not find a new passenger.

Just before departure he bought two Ceylonese, husband and wife and asked us to keep the small children with their mothers.

He collected KWD 25 per head from the passengers; we gave him only for 26 seats.

8:20 PM on 28 August 2012 the bus moved from Fahaheel to carry 40 Indian and 2 Sri Lankan person out of Kuwait.
The bus moved to Ahmedi Road, passing the Shuaiba refinery. Only the fire in the

Chimney of the refinery is the light in the whole area, there is no street light.

The bus entered into total darkness and moved through the desert road towards Jahra.

In half an hour time the bus crossed the Abdally border and entered Iraq. There is no border security, no visa formality.

The bus run smoothly and entered a small town filled with crowd of people, both men and women. Some army men were also stationed there. Three more buses are also stopped there. Someone in the bus said "Basra"
There is no light except the head light of the buses.
As soon as the bus stopped three four people entered the bus.

One man loudly asked "Do you have anything to sell. I will pay good price"

There was no answer. He asked the front seat passengers "Are you selling your wrist watch? Do you have any electronic items?"

One passenger said "I have only this, I need it"

The outsider lifts a bundle of banknotes and said 'See, I will pay you notes, I do not want anything free'.

Another person ordered the passenger "Remove you watch, give it"
The passenger was reluctant, but the person forcefully took it.

The first person argued with him "It is haram, return to the owner"
'Then you want to buy it' the second man said
The first person replied "I am not robbing, I am paying him cash"

I removed my watch and hide it under me thigh.

Fortunately, those two persons were quarrelling in front of the door, so no one else entered the bus.

I saw in the head light of the bus one woman is carrying a Cassette recorder from another bus and one man is cursing her. If he resists her and touches her, that man will be jailed for worse punishable crime, attacking a lady.

One boy was waiting there with food for the driver and his assistant. The bus was moved to 100 meters away from the crowd and parked. The driver and his assistant ate the food and handed over the lunch box to boy.

Then he took the micro oven of Salim and said to the boy "this is something new. Keep it at home".

Salim tried to stop him, but driver became angry and asked him "if I do not take it, the outsiders will take, do you want that"

We pacified him saying "We lost many things, more valuable. Let it go"

After 15 minutes we resumed our journey toward Bagdad. On the way, the driver stopped the bus at two populous areas to buy drinks for him. Before halting the bus, he warned us "Sit inside the bus. Do not come out. Otherwise you will lose everything"
He closed the door of the bus before he proceeded to the shop.

We reached Baghdad early morning; the driver parked the bus in the outskirt.

The driver said, "I will come here after 10'O clock. Here the life is normal and no one will trouble you. The shop will open after 2 hours; you can eat and drink then"

One asked the driver "Is there any public comfort station here"
"I do not know, Ask someone" he replied. "But be careful if any find that you dirty the road side you will definitely be punished"

Everyone, especially the ladies and children wanted to go to toilet. If the shops are opening we can go to any hotel, but no one is visible in the street.

Some people came out from their houses and stared us and left.

Then came a lady in her thirties and talked to us in good English. She allowed using the toilets of her house for the ladies and children. And gave them black tea in istican (small cups).

The pregnant woman in our team requested her to give the permission for her husband and his brother.

Reluctantly she gave the permission, not only for the two but all the passengers. She gave us some bread and said "I have only these. My husband went to Amman for his business. I am alone, that is why I hesitated to allow the males"

She talked about the government and the invasion. From her talk we understood she hates very much Saddam Husain and his policies.

At last she warned us 'You leave this place as early as possible, otherwise I will be in trouble"

So we left that house quickly, before leaving the house one passenger offered her some cash. She angrily shouted "What you think of me. I do all this for money. It is haram, I felt pity on you so I helped you"

Not only him, have several others also apologized to her.
We found a place selling bread and vegetable curries and ordered some. We got only half of the number of bread and little curry. The shop owner said "it is only for the people of this locality, not for outsiders. I give to you only because you are Indian"

I said thank to him and collected the food.

Faizy got two oranges from the next shop.

We were very hungry but food is very scarce. We cut the bread and gave bread with very little curry to each person. The oranges were given to children. This is the worse food we ate in our whole life.

"How sweet is the bread of Kuwait? Even dog will not eat this bread" one person said.

"Now our condition is worse than a dog" he added.

Around 11:30 AM the driver came with another person and said "I will stay here. This person will take you to Jordan. He is Jordanian"

We all entered the bus and the two drivers counted our heads. Then they went to nearest shop and bought something from there. The first driver left and second entered to bus carrying a bag in his hand.

He opened his bag and gave two apples and two peaches and full bread for all the children. Then the pregnant has him "Ahou, fee mai (brother do you have water"

He got down and brought one can of water from somewhere and gave her.

The journey was more comfortable than before and every felt that we were safe with the new driver.

Near the border of Jordan the military stopped us and asked the driver "who is inside"

He replied "qunood". Indians are known as qunood in their colloquial language.

The army ordered him to deviate to the nearest open ground in the no man's land between Jordan and Iraq.

The driver told us "do not feel bad. I am helpless".

Before he left, he gave the fruit and water to the children and pat one child and said "I have a daughter of your age"

From the no man's land, we were taken to a stadium in Military vehicle.

After throwing us into the play ground the military truck went back to bring the next batch.

It was totally dark and nothing is visible. It was not a grass court and the ground is made of loose sand like a sea shore.

Kamal said "let us occupy a corner of the stadium, keep our good and spend the night"

Faizy said "All are staying here. So better stay here. There may be desert snake hiding in the mud"

Shahuddin lit a cigarette lighter and in that flimsy light we had a look on the ground where we were forced to spend that night.

Shahuddin opened his bag and took a bed sheet. He spread it on the ground asked the ladies and children to sit on it. The children were very tired and went to sleep immediately. The two men with them opened a bag and took two bed sheets which were also spread adjacent to their children. Others also lay in the ground three four meters away, keeping their bags as pillows.

That pregnant woman said to her husband "achchaya, there is dew in the atmosphere. If you can, take a blanket to cover the children"

"How can I find one in the darkness, better you cover them with this bed sheet. We will sleep with the men" replied the other man in their group.

They both joined us.

Before dawn I heard two men are talking "If you want, go now to the side of the stadium before others can see it"

The other said 'my stomach is empty, I do not feel'

First man said "my stomach is paining, so I am going"

Second man said "wear your shoes, that area is filled with shit. There is no water here to wash"

Sun raised like a yellow ball in the sky, look like a shy lady covering the face with vale of snow.

Now we can view the entire stadium, thousands of people including women and children are laying there in the open ground.

My face was itching with pain and I asked Faizy to look at my face. He told me that the skin in the face is pealed like the snake skin, may be because of the dew of last night.

We found some acquaintance there, some of them from our town. They reached there two days back and struggling without food and water.

Ramachandran, one from our native place in India told "we are the most unlucky people, the people came here before us were allowed to go to Amman."

To our fortune, some Indian Embassy staff visited the camp around 10'O clock on that day. They checked the area and left.

Before they left they informed us that Indian Minister of State, Mr.K.P.Unnikrishnan will meet us next day.

John, the husband of the pregnant woman, narrated his experience when he tried to meet the Indian foreign minister, Mr. I S Gujral when he reached Kuwait one week after the occupation.

He was escorted to Embassy by Iraq Military and only rich Indians were allowed to meet him. When he returned he took with him those rich people with their belongings, leaving the sick and pregnant people there.

John concluded "Nothing will change to our pathetic situation"

Unexpectedly, before his arrival, two trucks reached with food and water. Each one is given a Sandwich and a bottle of drinking water.

It is given to all nationalities stranded there.

After one hour, one water tank was erected and a tanker filled the tank with the water.

Some canvas tents were also appeared there and there was a scuffle to occupy a bed space inside the rent. Medical team also arrived in the camp.

That night we slept like sardine in the fish mongers table, touching the bodies. Ladies were separated to another tent.

The man slept in the middle of me and the husband of the pregnant woman was crying with pain. He had high temperature and some swelling his face. He is a person from our neighboring state, Karnataka, from where only a very few people can to Kuwait. He was alone in that camp from his place.

We were taken to the medical team when they arrived around 10 O clocks. The doctor pronounced that he was suffering Chicken fox and shifted to the ambulance to transfer to hospital.

Hearing this news, John was very upset because "if I am infected with that disease, what will be condition of my wife and children." He started crying "I slept touching his body the whole night. It is fast spreading".

I was also scared because he stayed near to me.

As expected the Minister came there in the noon with a good number of Embassy officials and Jordanian authorities. He promised that we would arrange our repatriation immediately he reached India.

That day we got two time food, one sandwich each and water.

In the evening we tried to hunt for some food for the night. I and Salim approached the guards in the gate of the stadium. They seemed more lenient and told us nothing is available here.

We enquired "is there any possibility to go the nearest town?" The guard said "you check with the major, only he can give permission".

We were summoned to the major, a fair young man in his thirties, asked in a very tough voice "What is special for you. Thousands of people are staying here".

Salim told a lie to the major "my mother was seriously ill and I was planned to go to meet her. Then Iraqis came. Please allow me to telephone to know her condition"

The major was moved and said "You come after 20 minutes. One vehicle will to Jabal Amman. But you surrender your passport here"

We returned to the tent for taking our passports and money. Kuttan Nair also accompanied to us and the major did not object.

The vehicle dropped us in front of country restaurant in the outskirt of Amman. Then guard told us in Arabic "you can get good food here. I will come back after 1 hour"

We ate very nice food from that restaurant, at a very low price which we could not imagine in Kuwait.

The restaurant owner enquired about our condition and promised to arrange accommodation for one Jordanian Dinar per person in a day.

Salim told "we are 28 persons. Can u arrange'
He replied in broken English "Definitely, but each room I will put four cots"

He called a person to be an interpreter between us.

We told him that we were interested, but we wanted the permission of the major. He said he would talk to the guard who brought us there.

'He is a relative of mine, he will help you" he added.

Then we asked his assistance to telephone to India, he took us to a nearest shop. He asked us to wait outside the shop until he took the permission.

We telephoned to the house of my sister and informed our condition. There was no telephone in the house of Salim and Kuttan Nair. So, my brother in law promised to inform to their houses.

When the guard returned the restaurant owner explained to him. The guard replied "Insha Allah, I will take the permission"

When we returned to camp, the guard took us to the major, who returned our passports and asked us to go to our tents.

We hesitated and the guard told him about the accommodation offered to us by the restaurant owner.

"Let me think" the major said. After a pause he took the telephone and talked to someone.

He said "you three are allowed to go keeping your passports here?"

Then I told him "We are 28 persons including ladies and children".

He exclaimed "28 persons, I cannot allow that. I am sorry"

Kuttan Nair tried to get his pity "four children, one pregnant lady and another lady. There are diseases like chicken fox"

"I want to take permission. But you should stay in the same place." He said. He made two three telephones and finally said "ok you are allowed"

When we came back to the tent and told other members of our team, John raised several doubts

"How we can contact the embassy people? We will get the first chance to travel to India"

Faizy interrupted "If you want come with us. Otherwise stay here, we are going."
His friend said "It is government arrangement. God only knows when it will happen"

John's wife also asked to travel with us, so he agreed reluctantly.

At the gate the guard gave a plastic cover and asked us to put all our passports inside it and bundle it.

John again refused to give the passport of his family. Hence, we give the 24 passports in that plastic valet; fortunately the guard did not count.

The restaurant man accommodated us in four rooms and a hall. The two ladies and the four children occupied a big room.

Fortunately there was plenty of water in the three toilets and pipe outside the building. After washing and bathing, we ordered foods, nice foods at the cheapest price; everyone ate stomach full and slept.

CHAPTER 7

WE WOKE UP in the morning after a comfortable sleep without fear. Today is September 2, 1990, one exact month of suffering.

Some went to the restaurant for breakfast, some other ordered to bring it, and others did not want to spend for breakfast because they were afraid "What can be done if all the money is spent before we reach India"

After breakfast, we planned to go to the camp to meet the embassy people.

Kuttan Nair said "why do we all go there. If two people go there they can talk for all"

So, we decided that Salim and Kuttan Nair would go to meet the embassy people. John also wanted to go with them.

Jalal, who is superstitious, said "three is not a good number, either two or four start the journey"

Kutan Nair retreated from the plan, saying "let John and Salim meet them. I will stay here"

Salim said "I do not know much Hindi, Kuttan Nair must come with us to talk to embassy staff"
Kuttan Nair responded "all embassy staff know English, do not worry"

At last we decided that I should join to make the number four.

When we reach the refugee camp, the guards stopped us from entering. We had to wait there until the major came after two hours.

After entering the camp, we started searching any embassy staff to talk about our condition. All are busy and no one wants to listen to us.

Kuttan Nair said angrily "these donkeys do not want to help us. We will go directly to Embassy tomorrow"

We spent another 15 minute, and then I noticed a middle aged man getting down from a **limousine and walking to the medical tent. I followed him and said "Excuse me Sir" to attract his attention. He turned and asked "What do you want?"**

Salem narrated what had happened last night. He listened patiently and said "that is good news. I will send one of my men for investigation"

He was one attaché of the Indian Embassy who had the additional responsibility of the refugees.

We followed him to the medical tent. Some staff approached him immediately to wish him and report to him. There was a

lengthy discussion chaired by him while we were waiting in a corner.

John said "May be he has forgotten us. Let us go back. My wife and children are alone"

"Wait, let him come out" Kuttan Nair said.

After 10 minutes, the attaché came to us with two persons. He said "These two gentle men will accompany you. Show them all"

We said as chorus "Thank you sir, we will do"

These two staff brought a pickup van having eight seats with a carriage for goods.
In the van, they started to chat with us. They were Mr.Peter from Goa and Mr. Krishnan from Utter Pradesh. Mr.Peter was driving the van.

John who was usually silent started to talk to Peter "Peter sir, Peter sir, my name is John, my wife Elzy is pregnant and two children are with us. Please arrange to our journey to India in the first plane"

Krishnan replied "We discussing with the Jordan government. We will bring the plane once we get their permission"

John said "please give us the first chance, for God's sake"

These two gentlemen were satisfied with our set up and asked us "Is there any more hotels like this."

We took them the restaurant owner and introduce them. The restaurant owner asked them "how much you want and for how many days"

They replied "the maximum bed you can arrange for two months"

"I will tell you tomorrow morning. What about the food?" restaurant owner responded.
"How much will you charge for one time food, two rotties and little curry, chicken, mutton or vegetable?"

He said "normally I charge ½ JD, for you I can discount 50 fills"

Peter asked him "Can u discount a little more"

He said "Sorry sir, I will not get anything"

"We will finalize tomorrow morning" Peter said.

Next day, the agreement was inked; the restaurant man will arrange 300 beds, for each bed JD 1 for stay and 400 fills for one time food. The food will be served in between 12 noon and 2 PM only.

We went to nearest vegetable market. To our astonishment we found that one big basket of peach or apple cost only 1½ Jordan Dinar, which normally sold at equivalent of 7 or 8 Jordan Dinars in Kuwait.

We collected our passport with the help of the embassy staff.

After two days the embassy staff informed us to be ready to travel at any time. In the evening of that day, two buses came to the hotel to carry us to the Airport. At the same time two other buses came there with refugees to occupy the vacant beds.

We were asked to stand in a queue till the planes are ready, three or four planes were shuttling from Jordan to Dubai. Every half an hour one plane will take off from Amman airport with the refugees.

Thus we reached the third country, from Kuwait to Iraq, from there to Jordan, from Jordan to UAE.

Our plane landed in a corner of the airport and we were asked to wait in a separate hall in the airport building. We are given token numbers to avoid any scuffle to enter the next plane.

From Dubai airport bigger planes were servicing to take us to Mumbai. We do not know how many planes left before we reached there.

Around 9:00 PM we boarded in the plane to Mumbai and reached there around 3 AM on 6th September 2012.

At the airport our exit was arranged through a separate gate, every one paid Rs.100 and a train ticket to travel on a special train in the evening going to south.

There were a high number of volunteers of various organizations with food and other assistances to greet us, not discriminating on the caste or creed, state or anything.
We were startled to see that one Sikh religious organization offered bread and plantain knowing that we were not Sikh and not wearing the turban compulsory worn by that community.

We felt the homely feeling.

There is still time for the train journey. We went to nearest restaurant and took our breakfast.

Salim's co-brother is working in Mumbai and his brother is operating a travel agency there.

Salim Said "We will go to Hakkim Ekka and he will arrange the plane ticket for us. We are very tired. If we go by plane we can reach our place this evening."

Train journey normally take 3 days to reach our place, Varkala. There is one Indian Airlines plane going to Trivandrun at 2'PM and reach there at 3:30 PM. From there we can reach within 30 minutes by car.

Shahuddin's friends went to bring the rupees equivalent of the amount we paid to them in Kuwait. They promised to meet us after 2 hours at Dadar railway station, which is very near to the travel agency office. Now it is 8'O clock only, they will reach at 10 AM.

This is the same travel agency where I came before two years when my brother met an accident. I still remember my experience that time, hence I was reluctant to go there. Kuttan Nair also had a bitter experience from them, and hence he backed up.

Salim called Hakkeem, they both went alone. Before departing us Salim said "You come to Dadar Railway station. I will come there with the plane tickets"

Around 11'O clock Shahuddin's friends came and said to Shahuddin "We are very sorry that we cannot arrange the full cash in the short time. We brought only Rs.12000 which is enough for your plane ticket. We will send the remaining to you by money order"

With this money, we went to travel agency office, Faizy and Kamal went inside while others stayed outside.

Faizy returned back and said 'Salim Mama is not there. Nobody knows where he is"
Kamal continued "The tickets are not booked because they need the money first. Today there is no more planes"

Faizy said "let us try some other agency. We may get seats"

Kuttan Nair said "Now we have train tickets. The train will start at 3:30 PM from Dadar Station. It is very near to us. We will go by train"

Shahuddin supported him "We already travelled by two planes, we avoid the third one"

We decided to travel by train. Now it is noon time, we would take the lunch.

When we entered the nearest restaurant we found Salim and Hakeem eating delicious food. They were perplexed seeing all of us in the same restaurant. We sat in a separate corner away from them. They completed their lunch and went out without talking to us.

When we came out of the restaurant, Salim and Hakeem were standing there. Hakeem said to Faizy "Salim will come after two days. You go with others"

Salim continued "I will come there by plane after taking two days rest at Ekka's cottage"

Faizy was irritated and said "you do not worry about us. We will go today itself"

"If we go now we can occupy convenient seats" Kuttan Nair said. So, we proceed to the railway station.

Salim came with us till the railway station to see off his brother and nephew while we kept a distance with him.

At the station we met Mr. John, his bother and their families. They said the train will start from flat form No. 4 at sharp 3:30 PM.

So we moved to the train. There were very few passengers in that train. We occupied one bogie having sleeping berth to each one.

Hakim stayed outside the station, while Salim accompanied to us till the train. When we all entered the train Salim left. But before the train started he returned and said "the train is very comfortable, only very few passengers. Why should I spend money for plane?"

He also travelled with us.

In the train, some Malayalee association served us bread, plantain and water.

To my astonishment, I found people waiting in major railway station to help us with food and water.

When the train reached Ernakulam, only few passengers were left in the train.

At Quilon, we asked the driver to stop the train at Edava, a small station very close to our houses. The driver agreed and 13 people got down there.

Shahuddin is from Pallikal, a place nearly 30 kilo meter away from the nearest railway station, Varkala. It is nearly 9 PM and there is no bus going that area that day
Hence I asked to come with me to stay with me. But Kuttan Nair had a different proposal. He has a car running as taxi in front of the Edava Railway station. He will take five people with him and drop at our houses.

Faizy's house is just behind the railway station, eight persons went to his home.

I get down in front of my sister's house, in the main road.

As soon as the car door is opened, I heard a heavy cry "Misbah" from my sister.

She came forward and put her hand on my head.

I asked "how you know I am the person getting down from the car" Her husband replied "After receiving your telephone from Mumbai, she spends all the day and night in front of the gate to receive you"

I know how she loves all her brothers and sisters. For us she is not our sister but the person who took care of all her siblings since childhood.

I came to know that, when she hears the sound of the evening train, in which my youngest brother and his wife arrive from their work place, she will sit near to the front door looking the wall clock and if they are late for any reason, she will be agitated and arrogant"

Since the climate is moderate, we do not heat the water for bath and there is no water heater at any houses in that locality. But she insisted that I must take bath in hot waters to relief from the strain of the long journey. She filled the water in and a big vassal and poured boiled water in the vassal to get warm water.

After bath, I had the supper with all my favorite dishes, which is cooked specially for me.

She told me "you wife is in cosmopolitan hospital. Now it is too late. Tomorrow we will go there at 8:00 AM"

"Now you go to your home and sleep" she added. "your dresses are dirty. Leave all here."

Then she gave a new pair of dresses 'one shirt, one pants and one lungi'.

My youngest brother, you married recently also staying with her house. He has purchased the dresses for me. They know my dresses' size because usually they buy for me and send to me to Kuwait.

The bride is a doctor, she gave me some medicines, most of them are vitamins, after checking my BP, and sugar counts.

Sitting in the back seat of the motor bike of my brother, I reached my house around 10:30 PM. My mother in law and her cousins were waiting there to greet me.

The next day morning, I woke early and got ready to go to the hospital to meet my wife.

Then I heard the loud voice of my mother in law "the breakfast is kept in the table"

When she married to my maternal uncle and came to our family I was just four year old. She used to sing Muslim devotional songs as lullaby to make me and my younger brother sleep. Now, we are grown up, hence, as conservative Muslim ladies, she will not come to my sight.

My mother in law is a diabetic patient and very weak, her cousin sister is elder than her, but she is more energetic. She is childless and abandoned by her husband. Since all families in that locality are joined families, she is the eldest she is respected by everyone as head of the family.

After taking the food, I went to my sister's house. My other brothers and sisters came there with their family to meet me. They are all waiting me to take the breakfast.

I joined them and ate only 'dosa' with little potato curry.

After the breakfast, my brothers went for the duties and the children went to schools and colleges.

Now my three sisters and husband of my eldest sister were left. Husband of eldest sister settled in our home town after retirement from his work in Malaysia. His name is Hussain; we all call him Macha which mean brother in law of elder sister.

We hired a taxi and went to Trivandrum to see my wife, admitted in the Cosmopolitan Hospital. On the way, we picked up my mother in law.

Before we start, my eldest sister gave me a bundle of banknotes and said "Keep this until you take money from your bank"

I replied "I have only little money in my account. I could not transfer the money from my account there"

She replied "Do not worry, here there is no segregation as your money or our money. We are one family"

I know, she not only helps all her brothers and sisters but also controls all our activities. Even the children approach her for all their needs.

When we reach the hospital, Macha told "first the ladies enter the room and start the conversation. Slowly you tell about Misbah. Sudden news may raise her BP"

Myself and Macha stood in the corridor until my sister came out of the room and called us. I was bit nervous when I saw my wife, because of the fear that she might me tensed and increased her blood pleasure.

When Macha met the doctor, the doctor asked him "Tomorrow I have too much cases, Day after is not a good day and I am off. If you are ready we can take the children out on Tuesday"

By the phrase 'not a good day" she means the horoscope of the children born that day is not good near every major hospital some fraud astrologers have opened centers to take the advantages of the belief of people. Before Hindus were their only prey, but now people of all religions take their help to mitigate the misfortunes of the new baby. These astrologers are advising the date and time for taking the child from the womb of the mother . . . They will promise the bright future for children born at that time.

Since the patients are requesting, doctor have no choice. Some doctors are also superstitious and take extra caution to avoid bringing a child at a un auspicious time.

So, we decided to accept the babies on Tuesday at a time in between 10 and 11 AM.

On that day, all our close relatives gathered at the residence of my eldest sister and went to the hospitals hiring three taxis.

Here not only marriage, delivery of child, putting the ear ring to a baby all are festivals for the ladies, who are mostly housewives spending all their times inside their houses. Such occasions they wear new clothes and ornaments, cooks pastimes to carry to the celebrating house and spend all their saving, even borrow from relatives and neighbor

I was much trilled to see my two children and wished to shout that I am the proud father of two cute sons.

Because of a superstitious believe, nothing is arranged for the children before they come out safely. Now I want to buy everything.

There are several shops near to the hospital selling new born baby's good. I went to street joining cosmopolitan Hospital and G G Hospital, another famous maternity hospital.
The shops are open to the street and all the shops are run by ladies.

I stood in front of one shop; the sales lady asked me "boy or girl".
I replied "two boys"
She exclaimed 'twins, you are lucky. There are several couples praying for a child"
I did not like her talk.

She asked me the time of the birth, I told her 'in between 10 and 11 AM'.

She shouted "Kesavetta, between 10 and 11 what is the star"
Kesavettan replied from the room behind the shop "uttirittathy, good"
The sales lady asked 'do you want to write the horoscope of the children. Kesavettan is good astrologer. You can go from the back and meet him'
I told her now I want only the things for the children and I will think about the horoscope later.

She told several dress items' name and asked me "do you want this?"

Since I did not know what these items are I purchased two set of each and every garments she told me.

After accepting the payments for the sales, she reminded me "Do not forget the horoscope. My husband is a famous astrologer"

That is the story, husband and wife runs a horoscopy office and baby shop.

After collecting the good, my sister told me, one set each not enough. You buy another two sets" And she explained me what should be bought.

I went to another shop in the same street. The sales lady was very cordial and enquired about the children.

She asked me 'How are the boys. You are lucky you got two children at a time"

"How you came to know "I enquired her.

"Yesterday you bought the dresses from that shop. She told me" She replied.

"Is there anything unusual to discuss" I asked her.

"We are ladies, each delivery is news. All the operations are in the morning and people coming to us only that time. Afternoon we are free. We visit the hospital to see the new born children" She answered.

"Have you written the horoscope "she asked me?
I said "not yet"

She said "My husband is a good astrologer. The best in the street."
Now he has one client

I told her "I am a Muslim, I do not believe in it"

She said "Now all people are making the horoscope irrespective
the religion"
'Let me think about it' I said.
She requested "if you make it, come here only, do not go any other
place. My husband is the best"

I paid the bills and collected my good, turned back to return to the
hospital.

Then she asked me "who suggest the operation time"

While leaving that place I replied "the doctor, she is a good
astrologer"

My mother-in—law, my eldest sister and wife of my uncle stayed
in the hospital and other returned by night.

CHAPTER 8

A FTER REACHING HOME, I took the food and went to bed. My mind was filled with different thoughts:

Does my wife's health enough to feed my two children
How can she manage the two? How can I recover her health?
One child is very weak. What can be done for him? It is better they stay in the hospital for two more weeks.

I have to arrange someone to clean the whole house.

Where I can get good cradles?

At last my thought changed to financial problems.

I do have only a very low balance in my bank account. Is it enough for the hospital bills this is the best hospital in our locality, at the same time the most expensive one.

28 days after the delivery there are some religious functions to be observe. The major one is the 'removal of hairs' from the new born baby. If I hire a barber he will clean shave their heads, but there are other formalities to be taken before that. For boys, one or more sheep should be sacrificed and the meat should be distributed amongst the relatives. Gold chains should be rounded on the waist of the baby.

I do know the price neither of the sheep nor the gold ornaments. I decided to enquire it next day morning.

Next day, I woke up early and ate my breakfast and walked to my sister's house. Macha and others were ready to go to the hospital.

My sister came out and enquired me what I ate for the breakfast.

When we were alone; I asked her "what will be the expenses." She laughed and said "You do not worry, your macha have fifty thousand rupee you sent to him. If anything short we will manage".

'I have a small balance in my bank account" I told
She said "Keep it, you need it for your personal expenses until you go back to work"
Either she is optimistic that I can rejoin the same work or she said to console me.

My wife and children came home 15 days after the delivery.

There are a series of ceremonies to be observed to accommodate them

One room, adjacent to my bed room is cleaned and furnished to accommodate them.
Before that I and my two sisters went to nearest super market to buy two cradles and baby beds.

The first ceremony is 'tying the cradle', which is the obligation of the father's family. My sisters invited close relatives and came to my house with the invitees and the two cradle along with other things.

Second one is the removal of the hair and tying gold chain in their waist on the 28th day.

My wife's relatives want to celebrate the occasion lavishly because these are the children in their family after a very long time.

I told "I am jobless. No need to do it in such a grand level"

My sister intervened and told me "It is their happiness. We can celebrate as they wish."

Five sheep were brought, two for each and one for the food, and more than 100 people were invited. They were all feasted with delicious food.

When all left, I and my wife were left alone she enquired "why are you so gloomy".

I replied "Everything end up in grand. But I am thinking how we can feed our children. Nothing left with me"

'Don't worry, I have money in my bank account' she said.
'How much you have, how long will it last' I asked her.
'I have more than one lakh rupees, that is enough for more than one year'
'Wherefrom you got this much money'
'My savings from the money you sent to me' she said.
She continued "Ethatha will take my money only when her pension money and proceeds of the coconut sales finished'

She calls her mother Ethatha means elder sister, and her aunty, Ummachi, mean mother. Her father was working as Station Master of Kerala Transport Corporation, when he retired he got pension which was later transferred to her mother. Her mother will get the pension until she die and will be conveyed to their minor children if any.

"If you have that much, I will consult to any agency to arrange a visa to any GCC or Far East countries" I told her.

She got upset "you just arrived? You do not want to spend some time with your children"

"It will take more than 3 months to complete the arrangements. I will be with you until that time" I pacified her.

"You go after 6 months, not now." She requested.

After two days, my wife came to me crying "Ethatha is lying in floor and cannot move"

I called my sister in law, a doctor. She was ready to go to the hospital. She came within 10 minutes with her husband. Sadar. She asked me to take her as early as to Medical College or Cosmopolitan hospital, because she suspects a cerebral damage.

I informed Macha over the telephone. He and his wife came there with a taxi, we took to Cosmopolitan hospital.

She is the youngest sister of Macha and beloved sister in law of my eldest sister. Hence my sister is ready to serve her as a care taker, but we are afraid of her health also. We have to find out someone to help us at this moment.

My wife wants to breast feed my children; hence she cannot stay with her mother. We hired a caretaker from an agency in Trivandrum at a monthly payment of Rs.7000 for two months.

Two of our relatives agreed to stay in the hospital three days in a week in alternate period. That was a blessing.

My all three sisters finish their domestic works as early as possible and go to my house to look after my children.

Every day morning I go to the hospital by the early morning train and return in the last train. For that I took a rail season pass for one month. To spend the time idle is very boredom; hence I decided to do something useful

.

On investigation I found that Lal Bahadur Sastri (LBS) centre, an institute governed by Kerala government is conducting short time computer courses. I joined two of such courses, conducting in the early hours of the each day.

Later, I heard that Kerala government is opening a techno park and taking registration from interested parties to open any electronic business there. They will teach the prospective entrepreneurs and provide certificate to apply for the plot. I talked to my younger brother, Sadar, who was professor of an Engineering college. He advise me "that is better instead of going and suffering in the desert" So, I joined them and run after the project for a lot of time.

My children were crying every time and my doctor sister in law found out that they were crying because they were not getting enough milk from their mother. Next day she brought a carton of 24 tins of baby foods. The children stopped the crying. Every off day she went to my house and checks my children and spent thousands of Rs. for baby foods.

My brothers were shy to pay money to me, hence handed over money to my eldest sister when they get their salary payments, which she spent to meet the expenses of my wife and children.

My mother in law treatment last for more than one month and a good amount was spent from the saving of my wife. I am afraid that we are slowly moving to poverty.

To add our agony, my sister in law, Jehna came from Abu Dhabi, after a vehicle accident. Her one hand and one leg were plastered and her husband in the hospital in very critical condition. She is alone in her house in a very remote area, where he husband is working for the Abu Dhabi municipality as Supervisor. Without others assistance, she cannot move from her bed, hence her relatives decided to send home.

My co-brother has only his old mother and a brother as close relatives, but some distance relatives always meet him to get some assistance. His brother is also childless like him.

One of the distant relative who came there to get some money from Jahna said "all are because of the birth of these two children. Their horoscopy is not good"

My wife heard this and get her out of the house with warning do not enter that house again.

Every night, I go to my sister's house to tell them the present condition and take the supper from there, one day Macha told me one Saqir telephoned and said that he would come here next Monday by Vennad express reaching Varkala at 8:30 AM.

Next day, I called Faizy to inform that Saqir is coming on Monday to take his money. He replied that we will hand over the money before that.

I decided that I will go to the hospital Monday only in the evening.

Monday I went to Railways station to receive Saqir. We both had the breakfast at my sister's house. I telephoned Faizy and got the answer that he needs another two days to collect the money from others.

Macha was hearing my conversation with Faizy and enquired the matter, I explained to him. He told Saqir "I am going to Varkala and will be back after two hours. You stay here. We will lunch together and you can go by Parasuram express at 4:30 PM"

I and Saqir went to my house to see my children and spent some time there.

When we returned Macha came back withdrawing the money from his bank account.

We ate the lunch together and I dropped him at the railway station. He went to the North and I went to south by another train crossing at the same station.

After three days, Faizy came to my sister's house and handed over to Macha Rs.80, 000 and the remaining Kuwait Dinar. Macha did not tell him anything, may be because the marriage of his daughter with the brother of Faizy is discussing in between our two families.

I felt sorrow to know the fact that a retired man is wasting his pension funds due to a foolishness of mine in addition to meet a part of my family expenses. Kuwait Dinar may be worthless if Iraq continue the occupation.

My mother in law was brought back to home to continue the treatment. She could not eat any solid food; only take liquid food through a tube inserted through her throat. The medicine cannot be swallowed but injected into her body.

I hunt to find out a lady who can take care of her but in vain. At last I engaged one of my neighbors, who were an assistant in his uncle's hospital. He knows how to insert the tube and inject the medicine. He is jobless at that time and agreed to come to my house twice a day. I gave INR 20/—for each visit to him.

Now, my children start crawling and move freely. Now they want more attention.

One of the old servants of my wife house brought her daughter and said "she will stay here playing with the children". That girl is around 12 years old and as compensation her mother expects to meet the whole expense of her marriage, same we did for her. Her mother came to that house at the age of 11 and stayed there until my father in law found out a bridegroom for her and sent her on marriage paying dowry and gold ornaments. That person did not have a regular job; hence that wife and children were facing severe poverty. We render assistance on occasions

I started meeting people for arranging a new visa for any Gulf or far eastern countries.

One day I met an old classmate of mine in front of his hardware shop. My eldest brother arranged his visa and other formalities without collecting any money from him and met all expenses until he got a job. When my brother met the accident he called me from Dubai and enquired the condition and reminded me the assistance he received from my brother "Because of him, I am in this position".

Now he is a wealthy business man in Dubai and India. He also arranges visa for a fee of fifty thousand rupees.

As soon as I told him my requirement, he pretended that he was very busy and meets me after two day at the same place. We exchanged our telephone numbers.

I reached the same place at the prescribed time, but he did not arrive there. I telephoned him and repeated my requirement and added "I will pay your usual fees; I do not want it free".

He replied "Money is not a matter in your case. I am obliged to do it. But, I am not getting the visa as before. Already more than ten people are waiting for months"

I lost hope in his case.

Some friends suggested "you better go to Mumbai. There are several agents who can arrange visa for you."

I discussed the matter with Macha and my brothers, my brother said "now the war has started to throw the Saddam out of Kuwait".

He means the Operation desert storm started on 19 Jan 1991. Every time my mind was filled the development of that war. It ended on 28 February 1991.

Nothing is heard from company even after two months after the liberation of Kuwait. Again my joy had gone and grief conquered me. I telephone to my company several times but no one attended.

I am more worried remember the incidences before the Iraq occupation. I was substituting my immediate boss whenever he went out for official duties or vacations. When operation of my department was computerized I was more involved in the activities than him, which he feared. One day I was late for five minutes, he created the problem. He escalated the matter when one bank representative came to install their remittance system involving the GM and top management to this issue. The BP of the GM rose to a very high level; he fell paralyzed and was taken to Hospital. It happened nearly one month before the Iraqi occupation. I felt isolated because everyone blamed me on that incidence although they knew the real reason. They argued that I should respect their age.

I submitted my resignation from my work, but the management refused to accept it.

One day one Managing Director took me in his car to the hospital to meet the GM, who is convalescing there and is planned to shift to his home country Egypt for further treatment. From the hospital bed, GM called me near to him and held my hand and wept. He could not speak. It was on 28 July 1990, four day before the invasion. Fortunately he was carried to Egypt before the war.

My worry was the immediate boss, who worked the same company nearly 20 years more than me, had more contact to the management and he might have blocked me return.

I contact other employees of the same company to get any information. One Employee told me that Nathan collected all their Passport copy to arrange their visas. When I told that Nathan did not ask me and he said "Nathan sir will take only selected persons, definitely you will not be one among them"

After that discussion, I decided to go to Mumbai for trying my luck. I told this to my family. Everyone told me that money is not a problem, but we are all worried of you. We will also try for you.

My youngest brother told ': why do not you to start a business at the techno park' and every one supported him. Again I started my daily journey to Trivandrum.

When my railway season ticket expired, I asked my wife "Do you have any money in your account. I have nothing with me."

She said "I have only Rs.1800 in my account. I will take Rs.1500 and give you Rs.1000"
She went to bank and brought the money and handed over the money.

I kept the money over my lap and sat on the cot for some time thinking about the future. I heard the ringing sound of the telephone. I took the receiver and heard the happiest news.
The personnel manager of Al Muzaini exchange Company, Mr.Tareq Al Duhaim is on the other end of the telephone. He informed that my visa and air ticket had been sent by DHL two days before.

He traveled to Cairo Egypt to meet our GM, who suggested bringing me first to resume the business and he would join latter after complete recovery from his illness. He went back to Kuwait to arrange the visa for me and Mr.Saidu, another Malayalee working in the front office. With these two visas he traveled again to Cairo to send by DHL and telephone to us. Nothing was working in Kuwait at that time.

Next day I got a call from DHL office in Kollam and I went and collected the parcel.

There is no plane going to Kuwait from India, hence I have to travel to Mumbai and from there to Dubai, from there another plane to Kuwait.

I have Rs.1000 given me by my wife which is enough for a train ticket to Mumbai.

My brother said "you have to reserve the seat in the plane otherwise will be stranded at Mumbai"

I approached a travel agency at Trivandrum, East West agencies, run by my neighbors. They gave me the address and telephone numbers of their Mumbai office and advised to meet them. All the details are faxed to them and they would reserve the ticket.

In the night my wife said "I never took loan, I would give two gold bangles to my uncle to get a loan. How much you want".

I replied, "I have ticket, visa and Rs. 1000. Rs 750 are needed for the train ticket. I will manage with the remaining. Today Sadar paid the booking fees for the Air lines"

She said "you must keep some extra money. If you can travel the same day you have to rent room until the ticket is ready"

"I will take something extra from my sister' I replied.

Next day my brother booked the train ticket paying from his packet and sister gave me Rs.2000 for expenses.

My sister told me "If you need anything more call me. I will pay the money to Abdul Wahid Musaliyar and you can take it from his sons there"

Now my children are 10 month old and they had a special attachment to me. Whenever I am at home they stay with me. Now I have to stay away from them for a long time.

On that night, I lay in the bed keeping my children on both side of me and spent the whole night discussing to my wife on various matters.

Next day morning I started my journey to Mumbai.

That is the last time I met my eldest sister. She continued to look after my children after I came back to Kuwait. One day, she went to my house carrying some cookies and suffered cerebral haemorrhage. She was taken suddenly to the hospital, but doctors could not save her life.

That is the end of the life of a most affectionate person in my knowledge, who takes care of all her siblings like her children.

From the Railway station, I went direct to the East West travel office. That office is well known and the taxi driver dropped me in front the office

There are a big crowd of customers and I told the receptionist that I am referred by their Trivandrum office. She directed me to the first counter.

While I was standing there, Shihabuddin, the eldest of the owners came out from his office. As soon as he saw me, he came near to me and enquired. He invited me to his cabin and asked the counter clerk to follow him.

He enquired the clerk "What is the best way to handle this case"

The clerk replied "This ticket is taken at Airlines rate without any discount. Better we cancel this and take a new one at a much lower price"

Shihabuddin asked him "What will be the difference?"
The clerk replied "Nearly twenty two thousand Rupees"
Shihabuddin asked me "what is your opinion"
I replied "I brought only a small amount for one or two days' stay him"
He said "Money is not a matter. I take a new ticket and refund the old. The balance I will hand over to your home'

"Do it' he ordered to his clerk.

The plane to Dubai will start from Mumbai at 11:00 PM and we should report before 9:00 PM.

Now the time is only 12:30 noon, still there are 8:30 hours to reach the Airport. How I spend the time.

Shihabuddin was busy with the starting of their new airlines "East West Airline'. They got the operating license from the Aviation authorities that day. This is the first private airlines company in India.

He enquired 'Have you taken your food, I take early because of the meeting today'
Although I did not take any food except the tea from that office, I said "I am not hungry. I can manage"

He asked his attendant to show me the nearest restaurant.

"After food, you come back here. Ticket will be ready by then". He told me.

After the food, I telephoned to my sister's house and informed them the details of flight. My sister told me that my children are there and my wife will come there after ½ hours. She was here, now she went to feed her mother. I asked the condition of my mother in law.

She answered "it will take much time. Now her condition is much better. Jehna also need physical help now. So we keep the children here during the day time. In the evening we will take the children to Kadayil veedu'

I know this is practice even in my presence.

When I returned the travel office, it was past 3 PM and Shihabuddin enquired "where were you all this time. This is Mumbai, not Odayam"

I told him that I went to telephone booth after the lunch.

He introduced me to a person who is working as a news reporter for Kala Kaumudi news magazine. He is a native of Kalambalam, a place only 8 Kilo meters from our place.

'You both sit here, I have a meeting, after that I will join your company' Shihabuddin told us and left.

After 15 Minutes the clerk handed over to me the flight ticket and visa. He claimed Rs.200 for the service charges, which I paid.

I chat with the news reporter on the political and family matters until Shihabuddin returned at 4:30 PM.

He called the counter clerk and enquired about my travel documents.
He enquired "What else to be done"
The clerk answered "Everything has been arranged. Just go to Airport and take the boarding pass"

Shihabuddin told me "wait for ½ hour more. I will drop you at the airport'

He turned his face to the news reporter "Jaleel, Are you busy? We will go together to the Air port. I have something to share with you"

I, Shihabuddin and Jaleel started the journey to Airport at sharp 5:00 PM, myself and car driver were in the front seat and they sat in the back seat.

Shihabuddin said "Jaleel, We are planning to launch the first flight within two weeks. You can give this as news to your paper'

Jaleel asked him the details. He said "Initially two flights will be used, but in very nearly future five or six more planes will be added"

He added "I will provide you with the details within 2 days. We have to make some more arrangements."

'May I meet you day after tomorrow" Jalal asked.
'Today is 11 July, you contact me on 14 or 15" Shihabuddin said.

Then he turned to me and asked angrily "You do not know my relation with your brother, Vaheed. Why do not you inform me when he has an accident in my place?"

I replied "I was in Kuwait and came here only after two days"

"No body informed me, otherwise I do everything for him" he told me.

I know they were close friends and had a very warm relationship.

'Rashif and Kader know my office, why they do not come to me" he asked me.

I thought I should tell him the truth that they were not cared the welfare of my brother. But I told "I do not know why they do not come to you"

On the way, he directed his driver to a bar attached hotel. He ordered some nuts and a bottle of Whisky. The supplier poured the drinks in three glasses, and placed the glasses in front of us.

"I do not take liquor, so better you both share it" I refused it politely.

They urged to join them for a company; I said 'I never taste it so far. I do not want to start it"

After taking the first sip, Shihabudheen became eloquent and started telling his experiences when he stayed with my brother, Vaheed.

Shihabuddin talked in details about Vaheed's ability, his works, his business, his paintings and his miseries. I wish to know more about his life in UAE from the day he reached UAE in the year 1973 till him death in the year 1988. In those 15 years, there was a total change in his behavior. A vibrant and pleasant young man who was enjoying his life became a gloomy internally sobbing person. During this period we meet in the year 1984, when our mother expired and we stayed together for two days, mourning the loss of our mother. He talked about my future, but never allowed me to turn the subject towards him.

Unfortunately, Shihabuddin avoided my enquiries and slip the talk towards my second brother "jalal, I meet several people including film stars, but I can bet that few of them have the beauty of Safiyuddin"

He continued "Vaheed was very energetic and pleasant, but glamour vanished. He was struggling to sop his bad habits".
'Why he became like that" I enquired.

He did not answer me, but he asked me "Why Siddique is enemy of your family?"

Siddique is a close relative of me, son of my second cousin, I am not aware of his feud towards us.

"There is nothing like that, he is friendly with us" I answered.

He said "Jalal, Siddique married the girl proposed to Vaheed, he thinks it is a moral victory on Vaheed"

I answered "Ekka does not like that marriage although there is a serious proposal."

I did not tell him that some reliable source informed my sister that that girl have some mental problem, hence she does not allow that marriage. My brother did not attend the marriage and Siddique's anti used some sarcastic remark to my sister at the marriage hall, my sister did not attend the remaining ceremonies.

Shihabudin said Jalal "One girl has loved Safiyuddin, Siddique followed this girl and succeeded in molesting her"

I responded "it is not true."

Shihabuddin continued "He said not only these; he told me several stories about your family, especially about your cousin sisters. He explained me why he breaks his relations with your family"

"He talked all this because of his inferiority complex. He always compares his complexion and education with my brothers" I explained.

Shihabuddin said "I know it. Is he the same age of Safiyuddin" I answered "he is little elder, but he completed his secondary school with me, five years younger to him. He stopped his studies while we all studied up to post graduation"

Shihabuddin was tipsy; hence I did not want to continue the talk on our family matter.

But he narrated some incidence evidence his warm friendship with my brother Vaheed. Tears filled my eyes.

Jalal turned the conversation to their business.

Shihabuddin said "All arrangements were made and we will start it within 15 days. I wait for my brother Thahiyuddin to finalize"

Thahiyuddin is a close friend of my nephew Ahad, and many occasions I meet him and chat with him. He was in Delhi relating to license issues for the Airlines. I met his younger brothers, who were very busy with their works.

Thahiyuddin is the brain storm of their business; unfortunately he was murdered by underworlds.

I enquired about his other brother, Nasser; He replied "Now he is in Bahrain, He may reach Kuwait after 15 days relating to his business"

He reached Kuwait; unfortunately I could not meet him due to his strict schedule. I contacted him over telephone to find a convenient time for him, but he had no time to spare for me.

It is time to report to the Airport, Shihabuddin asked the bill. I tried to pay it but he did not allow it saying you are my guest, more over this the day for celebration for me.

At the airport, I said "I have some Indian Rupees with me; I want to convert some money to US Dollars"

He sent his driver to buy US$ 100 for my travel expenses. The balance I handed over to him, which was paid to my home along with the difference in the Air tickets after one week.

After taking my boarding pass, I said good bye to them and walked to the emigration counter.

CHAPTER 9

THE PLANE TOOK off at 9:30 PM towards Dubai.

I got a side seat in the middle row of the Gulf Air flight, but I could not recover my mind from the agony from the hypocrisy of my relatives. Siddique, a close relative of our family, talked very bad about us to an outsider. There is no known reason for it. He married a lady considering her wealth only. For that his family moved the things crookedly.

In the joined family set up we both belong to the same family, we both boost the nobility of that family, named Arasuvilakam.

Kader and Rashif are also members of the same family. For Rashif I spent from my hard earned income for two times visa and one time paid for his brother in law's visa. He should have shown some mercy towards my brother at his death bed.

Kader is my first cousin and I bring him to Kuwait. He was obliged to pay me more than KWD 3,000 for his visa and ticket and the funds I paid to his lenders.

It is the worst behavior of drunkards that they give preference to only to their pleasures than their relative's miseries.

In the plane, snacks were provided. After eating the snacks, I lay in the seat and slept.

The plane landed in the Dubai Airport around 2:30 AM, I have to wait for 5 hours at the transit langue to catch my plane to Kuwait.

I boarded the plane to Kuwait at 6:30 AM. The plane look like a military aircraft, not only the interior of the plane, but the passengers, most of them is members of US troops.

The plane took off at 7:30 AM

We were told to fasten the seat belt during the whole journey because there may be jerk when we approach Kuwait.

The atmosphere was covered by smoke from the burning oil pipe lines and there were several vibrations in the plane.

At last the plane landed in the Kuwait Airport safely at 9:40 Kuwait Time.

Military staff existed through green channel. There were many Kuwaiti Citizens, they were queued separately. Only six or seven Asian was in that flight, hence I could get out the emigration soon.

Fortunately there was one Kuwait Public Transport Bus outside the airport and I had coins to pay for the tickets. The driver told me that the banknote (bills) is changed and the old bills are no longer a legal tender. Only banks are changing the old notes.

The atmosphere is filled with smoke and the sun is seen in the sky like a full moon in the day time. Later I came to know that more that 600 oil wells were set on fire on their way back to Iraqi. The military in Kuwait is ordered to scorch everything in Kuwait to destroy Kuwait economy.

The road is wet from the last night rain. There are wild bushes in the sides of the road.

The month of July is the hottest days in Kuwait, but I feel cold when I sit in the bus. I am afraid that I may get fever due to the climate change. Mumbai was warm and Dubai was very hot.

Even in the Capital city few people were there and the city is still mourning the bad experience during the Iraq occupation. Some shops are burnt after looting, otherwise the city is intact.

My flat is darkened by the smoke; the doors to the balcony are kept opened. All the furniture is removed. Rafeeq told me that he sold the whole furniture and apparatus to an Iraqi, because he could not return to Kuwait. I owned a fridge, one cot, beds, one book shelf and few other things, that also were taken. My books were laying the floor partly wet from the heavy storm and rain, the water flown inside through the open door, opening to the balcony

I kept my bag in a corner of the room and entered the toilet. I opened the water tap, fortunately there is water. First water colored like tar came out and then clean water flowed from the tap. I urinate and then washed my face and hands.

I switch on the ceiling fan; the whole room was filled with dust. I get out of the flat after switching on all the fans and keeping all the balcony doors open.

I am very hungry, but only few coins are left with me. I have some Kuwait dinar old notes, but no one will accept it. Now it is not banking hours, hence I have to wait till next day morning to change the notes. I walked looking for a sandwich shop because I can buy two sandwiches with the coins in my possession.

I saw on Indian Restaurant, run by a person from our state. I asked him the price of one chapatti, the famous India bread available in Kuwait. Before the invasion, it worth 30 fills for each, now I am afraid what will be the price hike due to the situation. He said 50 fills per bread. I ordered two and paid 100 fills. He asked me "You don't want curry"
I said "No, not now, put some sugar over it". Sugar is free. While waiting for the bread, Adam, the last person I met before the invasion, came there.

He asked me "Hi, when you arrived"
"Before half an hour" I replied.

Then the hotel supplier brought my parcel. Adam asked me "Do you have money for the initial expenses"

I answered "I have only old bills; I can change it when the bank open tomorrow"

"Give it to me; I can change it at my bank. I can give new bills now" he said. He is working in Burgan bank.

I exchanged 12 one denomination notes. He said 'wait, we go together'. He ordered some chicken dishes and chapattis which will take much time. He told me "when you finish your food, my parcel will be ready"

A man I dislike very much is helping me at this critical time. That is life.

I ordered one tea and ate the chapattis and wait two three minutes for Adam.

On the way back to home, he talked only about him and his family.

"I do not go home, because I have been waiting for my son. Most of the expatriate students came to America from Kuwait are sent back to Kuwait. My wife and other children went to India with my relatives"

'I am satisfied that I have my son with me now and I can join my old job also. Now I sending my son as a trainee in the computer department of Gulf Bank, that is a luck"

He invited me to his flat. I refused it saying that I have to report my office before the morning closing and only 20 minutes left now,

Leaving him, near our residence, I walk towards my office.

Only very few vehicles are in the road. Looking on both side of the road to find out the damages made by the Iraqis and miscreants, I moved through my usual route for several years to my office.

A part of the heritage market is totally damaged. Except the concrete building all other buildings are flattered.

Iranians owned majority of shop in this area, hence it was popularly known as Iranian souq (market). Fearing the Iraqis, who are bitter enemies, they fled to their country. May be because of this reason, Iraqis destroyed these shops.

In my office only three staff and one person from owner's family was present. The three staff members are the accounts manager, Mr.Ramzi and two Iraqi brothers, Abdullah Atwan and his brother Riyad Atwan. The family member, Mr.Adel Al Muzaini welcomed me and took to his cabin.

He paid me KWD 300 and said "this is for your initial expenses. The company lost totally; otherwise I would have given to you a good amount. It is your responsibility to revive the company"

We came down to the first floor where my department is situated. I told him "it seems that nobody opened the door for the last 10 months"

He said "someone took two PCs from there. May be the watch man"

I started checking the equipments, the telex line not working, all but one telephones are dead.

The Reuters screen is not updating the news. My finger print is impressed in the dusty table when I touched it. The chairs are too dirty to sit on them.

I said "first we clean this area, I will find out someone to do it"
He responded: you do not bother, I will manage it in the evening"

"We will meet again this evening, better you go and take rest" he said and he left.

I took his permission to telephone my house and called them. I ensured that everything is well and fine there.

From the office I went directly to restaurant where I had my breakfast today. Now I have plenty of money on hand and at the bank. My family need money very badly, hence I decided to go to the bank before going to work.

The meal is not good, some rice and fish curry with one vegetarian side dish. I ordered the rice with chicken chilly fry. He gave me the vegetable side dish also.

After taking the food, I went to my flat. There is no vacuum cleaner available, so I cleaned a part of my room using a nylon brush I spread my bed sheet on the carpet floor and kept two books instead of the pillow and lay on it. I was very tired and sleepy, but hardly one hour is left before my office open for evening shift. There is no alarm to awaken me if I sleep. I started thing my future plan, first thing is to send some money to my family

Sharp 4 PM I reached my office, Saidu, a branch manager is waiting there. He is the other person who is called from India to arrange the things to commence the business. He was so happy to see me after a long time and came forward to hug me. He is very hungry because he did not eat any food since morning and he wait in front of the office for the last 3 hours.

I told him "the office was open till 1 PM and left that time. You came after that".

I knocked the door and the watch man opened it. We both entered in the office, he went directly to the toilet. When he came out from the wash room, we both went to the restaurant, leaving his bag in my cabin. He took his meal while I ate a snake with tea.

We went back to the work place,

When we reached there the accountant and the two Iraqi brothers were sitting in the ground floor. The accountant tells us that some labors are cleaning the two top floors, so better sit here until they finish their job.

Ramzi, the accountant started the conversation "Misbah, how you spent your holidays"
I responded "You were here during the occupation; you have better experience than us. So, first you tell us what has happened"

"After you all left, there are only few people in Kuwait. Food and water was scarce. We have no work. Simply sitting inside the house most of the time" he said.

Saidu enquired "What about the Iraqi soldiers".

"There is no military presence in Kuwait except some occasional patrolling by army" he replied.

I turned to Abdulla Atwan and asked "I hope, that you had a good time"
He answered "we are more afraid than Kuwaitis; they may consider us as traitors"

We chat for a long time. Saidu stayed in Kuwait until Indian Embassy in Kuwait arranged journey to India and they did not face any difficulty during their travel.

We heard a locking sound in the side door. Since the watch man was upstairs with the cleaners, Riyad Atwan opened the door. It was Adel Al Muzaini. He also joined our conversation, but said nothing about his bitter experiences. We know that he was hiding inside Kuwait fearing the army for several months.

At last the conversation turned to company matters.

Adel said "Fortunately, the safe is intact. They do not find out the valuable, especially the gold bars"

He continued "some official of one Swiss bank went to our chairman, Abdulla Ali and bullied him to occupy his house there. He wants to make a document pledging the house for their gold consignment

'He is the same person who worked for my uncle and destroyed all his businesses

I enquired "We have consignment of Credit Suisse and London Banks. What was their treatment?"

"The chairman contacted them; they all behaved sympathetically to him. They were ready to render all necessary assistance to him" Adel said.

"Now the biggest problem is that all the accounts are frozen and all drafts are dishonored" Ramzi said. "There is no way to contact the bank."

I said "one telephone is working; we can connect it to the fax machine also".

I asked Adel "Tomorrow morning, we check our license status with Central bank of Kuwait, and then only we work here"

He promised to come at 9'O clock to go with me to the Central Bank.

Central Bank is very close to us, and only a Car parking area and a mosque separate our two buildings.

Me and Saidu stayed in my flat that day and next day morning we went together to the restaurant and then to the office.

As promised he came at sharp 9 AM to pick me to the Central Bank. We met the banking supervisor, who enquired the present condition of the exchange.

The supervisor asked me "What are you going to do to solve the matter"

I explained "first I have to refund the dishonored drafts, then I have to reactivate all our accounts, we will pay for the gold consignments"

He asked me "What about the employees?"

Adel replied "We will bring maximum number of people. For the remaining, we will pay their indemnity"

He said "that is good, you do these things first, and then only we consider the license issue".

On our back, we discuss how we can contact the banks. I said "I remember an Irish man who came to me before the invasion to market a product called Comtext which is an alternative for telex. They have one office in Dubai."

"Try whatever you can" he said.

Only 12 telex connection hired from Bahrain Telecommunications were working through out Kuwait. These were given to major banks and imported government offices.

As soon as we reached our office, I called this company. Fortunately, they were very happy to serve us. They will send the software in two CD by courier 'Federal Express' along with the installation instructions.

When Adel left, I went to Al Ahli Bank of Kuwait to see the fate of the amount pending in my account. The balance is there, which can be withdrawn at any time. They amount given to me by Iraqi soldiers is not deducted from my account. For a moment I thought about John who was brutally killed when we both queued to receive the money.

I also changed the old bills with the new bills. I send all the balance in my account to my brother in laws account by telex transfer. They refused to add the cash in my hand to my balance. But, I am happy that I receive nearly 4 times Indian Rupees as counter value of the amount. Not only that, but also my family will get the money to meet their living expenses within the next two days.

I collected the details of all our accounts and prepared letters to each and every correspondent banks and exchange companies.

Now the question is how I can send these letters. There is no postal system in Kuwait. Some has to travel to neighboring countries, Saudi Arabia or Bahrain to send letters.

Fortunately, I received the CDs from Comtext on the second day. The instruction for installation is very clear and easily graspable. When I found the system working fine, I shouted loudly as if I had invented something great.

Hearing my loud cry every one came to me and enquired. I answered "90 per cent of our problem is over, the rest I will complete in a week's time"

I continued "From today onwards we will process all the unpaid drafts. We will discuss the mode of operation for it: now'

Abdullah Atwan said "Most of the people bring copies of the draft and some of them hold the original draft itself"

I advised "we will not refund any cash for the draft amount. We will issue replacement cheque only after receiving confirmation for cancellation from the bank"

"What documents will be given to the customers?" Atwan asked.

We switch on the server, fortunately it is working. So, we can give the customers receipt for commission with the full details of the draft.

The next thing is to decide the commission for cancellation. We heard that the banks are changing twelve Kuwait Dinar, hence we fixed the commission as 8 KWD.

In the evening, we opened the front door for the customers only to accepting the old draft copies for cancellation. We promised one month time for replacement draft.

First day, nearly 100 customers approached us and we were able to close the counter in time.

When the work finished, we get out of the office. In the inclement climate we walked to our flat. One person is waiting there for us.

He said "the rental contract of the flat is not in your name. So, you should not stay here".

I told me "I am staying here for the last three years, the watchman knows it. You can ask the watchman"

He said the watchman returned to his native country Sudan and he died there.

I showed him my old civil Id which shows my residential address clearly "See my address in my battakka madania. The flat address is written here"

He replied "then you make a new rental contract. The rent is KWD 250 per month".
I said "before it is KWD 90 only, why you increase to this high amount?"

He replied "You are an old resident; otherwise I will collect KWD 400 per month"

There is no benefit to argue with him. So I said "I will come to your office within two days"

He said "Only two days, third day I will come and vacate the flat"

I discussed the matter with Saidu, and we started checking for a flat.

We asked the restaurant owner to find a flat for us. He had an alternate suggestion; he will rent one room in his staff quarters for us. Including 3 times food, he will charge KWD 60 per month.

Since such kind of stay, known as mess. is very popular in Kuwait. We have experienced the bitterness of the system before; hence we decide to try for another set up. In one room there will be five or six persons and quality of food given to the inmates are very poor.

Still we have two more days, so we decide to search an accommodation after the working hours.

But, the things changed when we reach the office in the next day. A long queue is seen in front of our office before the opening. They all came to exchange their dead draft with new ones.

We both had a hectic time and could not come out of the office before 11 PM. We have no alternative now, but to agree the restaurant owner's proposal.

It is not a room, but an open space in the ceiling of the restaurant. A part of it is used as the store of restaurant and the workers are living at another corner.

He asked his workers to move the things from the other side of the structure and put two cots there for us. We paid to him money to buy two beds and pillows from another city, Hawally.
We vacated the flat and moved to the new shelter.

The very next day two more people also joined us to share that place. They are unknown to us, and become prey to the restaurant owner under the similar situation of us.

Before the invasion, that shop was a textile, the ceiling room was a tailoring shop, attached to the textile. It is a low floor structure; anyone can touch the roof if he raises his hand.

The hall is dark even in day time, and a neon bulb is always giving light to us. Two air conditions are placed in two corner of the hall. There are ventilations of 2 feet long and 1 foot height on two sides of the outside wall to bring inside oxygen. The entrance to the hall is through a very narrow metallic ladder placed inside the restaurant.

One corner of the floor there is a toilet with a European closet, but there is no shower to take bath. We fill the water in a plastic bucket and pour it over our body with a mug.

I am the first person who gets up from the bed and ready to go to the office. Saidu will be in the bed when I reach the office. Until the office is open for customers at 8:00 AM he has nothing to do. I am alone in the back office and international department; I have a lot of work to be completed as early as possible.

The number of applicants for stop payment of draft has multiplied several folds and I have to process these applications. I am making the correspondents to our banks to reactivate the accounts. More over I have responsibility to rearrange the infrastructure to be ready to recommence the business at any time.

It is only 5:45 AM when I start my journey to the office. Although the sun rose one and half hours before, it was dark. The atmosphere is filled with smoke. Last night there was loud thunder and lightning, but there was no rain. I walk through the street as I search my way in the midnight nobody in the street, which is normally filled at this time, with vehicles and people before the invasion.

The air is very heavy filled with smokes socked in oil and I sweat due the hot wind. My dresses are wet as if I take a bath in the tar. I feel uneasiness and suffocation.

I knocked the office door and wait there more than 5 minutes. Since there is no response from inside me knocked more loudly. The watchman opened the door, rubbing his eyes. He is not happy because I awakened him too early.

As soon as I entered my cabin, I removed my shirt, which has been white but now the color is changed to dark black. I sit on my chair and start work. I know no body will come there for the next few hours.

There are plenty of works; I am totally confused to give preference to which particular work.

I opened the cabin of Mr.Surendra Nathan who was my immediate boss before the invasion. I took the banking relation files one by one and read.

To my surprise I find the file of State Bank of India, The account with this bank was closed in the year 1981, but the balance of more than 200 Million Indian rupee is laying there in the bank. This amount is worth 700,000 Kuwait Dinar before the invasion which is now diminished to 220,000. What a loss? At that time one

Kg of Gold cost only 375 KWD, hence this amount is worth 1870 Kilo gram of the precious yellow metal.

Why this amount is left idle for more than 10 years? State Bank of India is asking only a bank guarantee from any local bank that they will be replenished if any one claim on this fund. Instead of providing them a guarantee, there was an attempt to transfer this money to some Indian Expatriate in Kuwait. Why? Is it an attempt to embezzle the funds? To whom I will ask? No one is here to answer me.

The company is facing very big financial crisis at that time because of the share market crash. The company is paying interest much more than their annual profit.

I continue my checking of files till 7 AM. I found several inappropriate way of handling the company funds. It is managed properly; the company can avoid interest payment of millions yearly.

I found one advantage that all the company's accounts with foreign banks were running with substantial credit balance, hence there is no requirement for money to operate these account.

Now the only problem left is settlement of the gold consignment by Switzerland banks which need a lot of money. There may be good demand for the gold in the nearest future, but they won't wait till then.

If we resend the gold back to them, a huge amount should be paid for insurance, Kuwait is considered as a war zone. Also there are no airline companies who accept such kind of parcel. So, we decided to buy that gold if any of our account which has enough funds to pay for the gold can be activated soon.

Fortunately, we were able to unfreeze our account with our American correspondent bank, Irving Trust Company, New York. That was a major step forward.

Banks in Europe and Asia reopened our account, except Indian banks which are waiting for Reserve Bank of India approval. Reserve Bank of India is refusing the reactivation of the account due to a misunderstanding and wrong information received from Indian Embassy in Kuwait.

The previous chairman of the company took his shares and opened a new company with a similar name and actively doing share business by bringing some dealers from a Swiss bank. That company collapsed miserably making him the biggest debtor in Kuwait. Indian Embassy erroneously mentioned our name as the bankrupt company to the Reserve bank of India.

By the by, two of the dealers from Switzerland bullied our chairman at Geneva.

The biggest issue in the Kuwait Banks, all are refusing to reactivate the account without paying the amounts due to them.

The company has to pay big amount of nearly 28 million Kuwait Dinars to a consortium of banks headed by Commercial Bank of Kuwait under the Difficult Credit Facilities Resettlement program. The consortium was formed to assist the financial companies suffering from the "Souq Al Manakh" collapse in the early 1982.

Souq Al Manakh collapse is the second blow to Kuwait Ecnomy in two years, just after the beginning of the Iraq Iran war in 1980. Souq Al Manakh is the unofficial share market run parallel to the official stock exchange homed in an Al Manakh, mean CAzal Sitting. It is an air conditions shed used for Camels, which later became a financial hub for exchanging shares by the low income group of people who has no previous knowledge or experience in Share trading. It is considered as the biggest speculation in the history and in the peak days it is ranked as the third stock market in the work, next to USA and Japan. The whole operations are conducted by post dated cheques and the total volume of such dead cheque is estimated to US $ 94 Billion.

Nearly 6000 Kuwait citizens are involved in this speculation, among them some from the Muzaini Family are great players. This incidence brings not only shame to the company, but big loss for holding a very high volume of post dated cheques which will never be paid.

Everyone expects grand level of support from the government similar to the intervention in 1978 to correct the minor financial issues in the official Stock Market., which is mainly operated for the highest level of citizens like members of the ruling family, rich business man, high rank government officials. But there is no assistance from the government, except some minor control from Central Bank of Kuwait.

Commercial Bank give an option to my company that the funds can be repaid in three installments, KWD 12.5 Million immediately, same amount again in the next month and the remaining amount plus the outstanding interest amount in the 3rd month. We have no alternative but to accept their conditions to satisfy the Central Bank of Kuwait.

Around 2:30 PM Saidu came to my cabin and said that he took half an hour rest for lunch and asked me to join him.
I just closed my cabin and went with him.

On the way to the restaurant, Saidu said "see, the top floors of Kuwait Finance house is covered by clouds'

I said "It is not cloud, but smoke."

He said "Surely it is both; there will definitely be rain with thunder in the night. We should leave the office earlier today"

He continued: "there are more than six thousand stop payment request today. I will send these to you as soon as I reach the office"

"That is a very heavy work, I have no assistant, I don't know when can I finish it" I responded.

We ate our lunch and returned to the office. On our way back we heard the heavy thunderous sounds. The clouds are in very low altitude, the tremendous sounds pained our ears, like a sharp weapon is piercing though them. We moved very fast to reach our office before the rain.

.

Even in this bad climate, there are several customers inside the exchange company. Most of them want to buy new drafts and a few of them came to replace their old drafts with new.

Now we have not accepted new customers, the only thing we are allowed by the Central Bank is to issue draft in lieu of unpaid drafts during the Iraqi occupation.

I carry some of the applications from the counter to my cabin and asked the watch man to help me to bring the remaining.

At my cabin, I take some applications, sorted it into bank, then again in the currency of the draft amount.

I made a template having a table with columns for draft Date, No., currency name, amount and drawer branch. This made my work easy and I succeeded to pass the stop payment instructions for more than two thousand application in four hours time.

Now it is 8 PM and the front door is closed. Saidu comes to me, but I am still very busy with my work.

"Better you go, I will be very late" I told him.

He said 'better you come early'

I said "then wait for 15 minutes, I will finish the present task" Ramzy also come to me and says "there is heavy rain outside. We cannot move now"

I requested them 'better you assist me. Sort these papers bank wise"

They are very tired but they do not avoid me.

Around 9:30 PM the watchman came and said "now there is no rain. Better you reach home before the next rain"

We left the papers on the table and left the office for the day.

CHAPTER 10

NEXT DAY I came to office at 5:30 PM. The atmosphere is clear because of the last night rain. After a break of half hour when we walked to our residence, the rain resumed that night. It last till the early morning.

The road is still wet, the carbon and oil mixed in water painted the road and buildings in black.

Since there is only little smoke in the atmosphere, sun is visible in full shape with moderate heat. These days the sun rises at 4:00 AM, but hides in smoke throughout the days.

I forget the decision me and Saidu taken last night to cover our face with a towel when we walk in the street. The face is creamed with the mixture of carbon and oil that not only irritate us, but also the stain cannot be removed even by a bath with soap.

The watch man opened the door at my first knock and I entered the building.

There is no news, no news paper, no TV and no internet. No radio is broadcasting English news. I felt totally isolated. Even my colleagues talk about the work only.

I telephoned my house and enquired their whereabouts. Then I asked them "Is the world still there. I have no idea".

My wife laughed and said "why are u thinking like this"

I asked her to take the news papers of last three days and read the news heading. I spent nearly 10 minutes holding the receiver. I am relieved because there is nothing wrong done to the earth.

I started my work and continued till 9:00 PM without break. Saidu brought two Samosas, an Indian snack, when he returned after lunch that is my lunch for the day.

In the evening the atmosphere became cloudy and around, 7 PM there is heavy pouring with loud thunders, which forced us to stay inside the office.

When there was lull in the rain, Saidu told "better we go now, otherwise the rain will strengthen, and we cannot reach our residence"

When we reach the restaurant, we are totally wet, we changed our dresses. I brought five set of dresses for office and two night dress. Now all are dirty and we cannot find a laundry.

I lent a plastic bucket and took some soap powder from the kitchen. I washed my cloth which is already changed the colour to black.

Days passed like this; at last we succeeded to get the approval of Central Bank of Kuwait to resume the operation in the first week of August 1991, under the condition that the loan of the Commercial Bank will be settled within one month.

Plenty of money in our account with foreign banks because they do not honour any draft after the invasion. Now, we can issue more draft on these accounts. That is a great advantage.

Those who stayed in Kuwait during the occupation hold a huge amount of money, which cannot be sent to their home country. Commercial Banks will not accept any fund by cash and transfer.

Now we are the only Foreign exchange Company in Kuwait. Telex transfer is not popular at that time and the post office system is not efficient. Only option left with the people is buy a draft and send it by post, which will reach the destination after one or one and half months.

I made a suggestion to utilize the funds collected from people for draft for settlement of the loan. We can recoup the funds slowly. Everyone agreed that and the full loan were settled immediately to avoid further interest payment. Also, we utilized some funds to buy the gold kept with us as consignment. We are worried that the price of gold may come down when the tension in this area recede. Fortunately it happened other way; we got a very good profit when we sold to a Saudi Jeweler after three months.

Since there is no competition, we take a very high margin, little lower than the banks. The volume of business is very high that enable us to run the show with good profit and without any liquidity issue.

With the skeleton staff, the company managed to open one more branch at Hawally which doubled the business volume as well as my work load. Every day I reach the office before 6:00 AM and leave after 10:30 PM, this became a routine.

The company is not paying any interest for loans, charged at 12.5 % with amount to around KWD 4 million yearly. That was the biggest gain.

One Kuwait National, who works in our department, wants some workers for his and his relative's house and business. Unfortunately, I had only the details of two persons, which I gave to him.

Before I returned Kuwait, my cousin, Kader gave me the passport copy of his eldest son, Aslam. This boy is not even completed the primary education and not trained in any trade. Hence, we cannot get a job better than the watchman of an agricultural form.
The other one is Shahudheen, who traveled with me when we flooded from Kuwait during the Iraqi occupation. He knows driving; he is employed as a driver.

Aslam is a wrong choice; he is scared to sit in alone in the night, while other guards are sleeping the room attached to the gate. He is not getting the Indian food served to him by his mother.

He behaved as a mentally sick man at the work place and his employer brought him back to my residence. I tried to keep him with me and find another job, but he insisted to go back home. Not only I paid compensation for the losses of the employer to get the passport, but also I arranged his ticket and other expenses to send him back to India.

Shahuddin has another problem; his old employer noticed that his very young third wife is mingling very closely with Shahuddin. The jealous husband terminated his service, but he will pay the passport only after paying KWD 500 for the visa and two years residence. I lost that money also.

The next task is to open the other branches, for that the old employees should be brought from their home country.

Giving the staff file and some letters, Mr. Tareq Al Duhaim, the personnel manager told me "Misbah, you choose 12 staff from this for working in our branch and 3 for other departments. I will apply for their visas day after tomorrow"

Since it is an urgent work, I spared some time for selecting the people. Saidu came to know this and asked me to select some of his relatives, who were working in the company for a long time.

The first thing I noticed a parcel received by courier, and I opened it. It is sent buy Mr.Surendra Nathan, my ex-boss and containing more than 20 passport copies of old employees as well as new applicants with their bio data. I read the covering letter, which gives advices to Mr.Tareq such as do not call Misbah and Varghese, he will train the new workers to be better than Misbah, he will rearrange the things and make it work better than before etc.

I selected the 15 staff, leaving the persons recommended by Surendra Nathan. But I showed the letter to Mr.Tareq who agreed to my decision to avoid those persons

We, the four inmates in the ceiling of the restaurant jointly hired a flat in Sharq Area and shift to there. We shared the cost for purchase of all appliances for the residence and arranged a comfortable accommodation. We are planning this sine the first day of entering this accommodation, now two things prompt us to do this now:
The previous Friday, we travel to areas where our friends and relatives were staying before the invasion and returned 3 PM. The restaurant owner refused to serve the food because we were late. He had an unexpected number of customers on that day. Many people had returned to Kuwait in this short span of time.
Second thing, more staff will join us and we have to accommodate them until they make their own arrangement.

That was a two bed room flat with a long hall, having a kitchen and two toilets. The rent is KWD 110, which is affordable.

More people from the home village of Saidu, some of them are his relatives, returned to Kuwait. They all need a temporary shelter until they find out a convenient one, hence stayed with us in that small flat. Fortunately the hall of the flat is big, one side of it a dining table is placed and in the other side a cot is lying. In the middle of these two, 15 to 20 people can sit.

The first three floors of this building are hired for business offices, the tea boy cum key holder of one of this office is known to Saidu. This office is functioning now, but the tea boy is living inside the office. In the night, he will allow 20 to 30 people to sleep on the carpet floor of his office. We purchased some bed sheet and pillows for make their stay comfortable.

Before November 1991, we restarted the operations through all our existing branches. With the increased business the company was able to take more float, which not only covered the funds paid for repayment of the loan, but also placement for new deposit.
I noticed that the balance in the company account with some banks is increasing day by day, which means that there is much delay in encashment of our draft. So, I consulted with some banks to accept short term deposits from us and they agreed. Thus the drawings on these banks will not be covered in the account the very next day, but the equivalent in US$ will be deposited with the same bank for short term to gain the interest. At the maturity, the bank will credit the proceeds to our US$ account with them.

Now, the risk of exchange variation must be mitigated, which is solved by selling the US$ forward value date at premium to the same date of maturity. Thus we had additional gain on swap

Now the company rejoiced after a very long period of struggle with funds issues, loans, interest, etc.

The company also gained very high amount from the operation for the four months up to December 1991. Coupled with the profit from the gold sale, the company is able to recoup a major portion of the customer funds used for the loan settlement.

Three more companies renewed their licenses and restarted the operations before the end of the year 1992.

The winter season started from October with chilling cold much higher than the previous years. There is a scarcity for winter dresses, especially office jackets, but all are looking for something to keep the body warm.

Now the plants in the road sides of Kuwait are blossomed and the butterflies, which are never before seen in Kuwait, are spreading their small wings. There is rain daily and bushes have grown in the open areas. There is a total change in Kuwait.

An American company is working for the last three months to put out the fire in the oil pipelines and the atmosphere is clearer than before.

We started the 1992 on fresh note to enhance the business to utilize the favorable situation in this country. In addition to the existing 8 branches, we opened branches at our major commercial centers in Kuwait as well as added more correspondent bank to cope with the change of expatriate communities in Kuwait after the liberation.

Some countries like, Bangladesh and Egypt, helped Kuwait in the war for liberation by man and these entire mercenary were given employment in other sectors. They brought their friends and relatives resulting in a huge increase of this population. White skinned women from Philippines, Indonesia and Nepal are recruited in tens of thousands to work in the houses, restaurants and shops. With them some males are also came here.

I requested Mr. Tareq for a favor "My brother is working as an officer in University of Kerala. For a long time he is requesting me to bring here. Can u employ him?"

He said "Misbah, I am happy to bring your brother. Bring his passport copy"

I gave him the passport copy, which I kept on valet the day before.

After getting his visa, he applied for leave from his present employment and joined me after 50 days.

Now my work load is too high to finish it in the same day and pending works are accumulating. I really want an assistant, but I have to wait until the old employees return. I work minimum 14 hours daily and struggle to maintain my physical and mental health.

One day, Mr.Adel Muzaini bought a young woman, graduated from Kuwait University just be the Iraqi invasion of Kuwait, to assist me. I was not happy because of the Arab Ladies are normally troublesome, when they work with other nationals. As a preliminary assessment of her ability, I asked her to sort out the papers and record in a register, which is completed by her within a very short time.

Convinced by her performance, I asked her "What is your name" She replied "Azal"

I asked her "Do you have any idea about computer, can you type" She said "Little"

I showed her how to input the data in the system and asked her to do it when I am busy with other works. She exhibited exemplary ability to grasp the task and execute in a very short time.

We both were very busy and there was no casual talk or introduction for the first two weeks.

When she got her first salary she brought some Arabic sweets like Falooda, and gave to me.

I said thanks to us while noticing her new dresses. She was wearing shabby dresses from the first day of joining and talked very little about her personal matter.

As an introduction I talked her about me and my family with the ambition that she will reciprocate in the same way, but she said nothing. I do not want to ask her personal matters, hence our conversation end there.

When Mr.Abdulla Atwan met me the next time, he asked me my opinion about Azal.

I replied "a nice and very capable girl"

He became eloquent after hearing my worlds, "She is a marvelous girl, and she is first in her school and college, overcoming all the hardship in her young age"

He continued "She is a bedoun, no fixed area of settlement. Her mother married to a rich merchant of Iraq, one of his several wives. He put her in a house near to Basra in Iraq where she became pregnant, delivered this girl and become widow two months after delivery. He has grown up children in the first marriage, but their mother is controlling the things. She brought her brothers and throws her step sister and daughter. Scaring their abuses, Azal's mother run to Kuwait".

I asked him "why they deprived her share of her father's wealth. Is it not a legal marriage? Was her mother a paramour of that person?"

He answered "It is a legal marriage registered under Islamic law. But the brothers of the first wife are very influential. Azal's bothers want to help her, but their mother will not allow them"

I asked Him "How they survived in Kuwait without any assistance"

He replied "Her mother has a distant relative in Kuwait, named Yousef. Hearing the news we went to Iraq to assist her, but he could not find a solution due to the adamant attitude of the step sister and her brothers and then he brought them to Kuwait. He is a truck driver working for a local company and has no children. He supported Ummaima, the mother of Azal when she was young. Ummaima was an orphan, may be the daughter of a fifth or sixth wife of any womanizer, who abandoned them when he find another."

After a pause he continued, 'The relative of Ummaima arranged her marriage and collected the dowry which Yousef spent fully for Ummaima. He was very much sympathetic to Ummaima and accommodates her in his house. His wife, Ummulkulse treated lovely to the lady and her daughter. Ummulkulse is a street vendor of inner garments and indigenous medicines. When she goes for work, she will take Ummaima and daughter.

After sometime, she opened other outlets and gave the charges to Ummaima. Before two ladies take care of the child, now they are in two separate places. The girl walks in the street. The ladies are worried of her. Yousef find a solution, to admit her in the school where she will spend her time till noon.

Noticing her brilliance, the teachers and some natives encouraged her and advise her mother to teach her the maximum she can. Yousef treated her as his daughter and in his free hours he takes her out for shopping and sightseeing.

Once Azal asked him 'Can you teach me driving" Thus she learned driving and Yousef arranged the driving license for her.

They were leading a very happy life until the death of Yousef in a road accident. Since, according to the Muslim custom, Ummukulse must observe "Iddah—the period of waiting" cannot show her face to any men for four months and ten days after the death of her husband, Ummaima goes for the business alone.

A wicked person, Hairone started disturbing with the promise of marriage and persuaded her for adultery. Fearing his sexual advance, this lady suspended her business until Ummulkulse complete her Iddah.
Now, Hairone starts visiting the residence with presents but the house always closed against him, which makes him angry and threatens the two helpless women. Now Azal is a grown up girls and reached the marriage age of Bedouin community.

Hairone is working for the Jahra Municipalities, hence capable of file a case against these two ladies for street vendor without proper license from Ministry of Commerce and Municipality.

Smelling a rat in his words, the two ladies decide to shift the business to another governorate, but Azal suggests going to Women market at Kuwait City Heritage souq. Azal has a car presented to her by Yousef and she agrees to drop these two ladies every day at the Women Market.

During the Iraqi occupation of Kuwait, they struggled very to find out their food and Ummulkulse became ill. Despite her illness and fatigue, she walks five to ten miles to find some food by doing any filthy work. After the liberation of Kuwait, she meets several people to get a work in respectable office for Azal, which is the last ambition of her deceased husband. He always says his acquaintance that his granddaughter will be an officer in a bank within two years. Like majority of citizens in Kuwait, she consider foreign exchange company as bank, hence go every day to Muzaini family requesting a job for Azal and at last persistent hard work find the fruit and Azal joined in Al Muzaini Exchange Co.

Tension mount in Kuwait and a section of Kuwait Citizens started challenging the authority of ruling family. After the liberation, the Amir agreed for the National Assembly election in 1992 under international pressure. The opposition group won most of the assembly seats and the unchallenged power of the ruling family is controlled.

There are fifty elected members in the assembly from twenty five constituencies and up to 16 officials, mostly nominees of the Amir will add to this numbers. The maximum number of voters in a constituency is less than 10,000 which means 90 % of the total population have no voting right.

There are more than 600,000 Shiites who is considered as second class citizens by the majority community, Sunni. Nearly 2/3rd of business community in Kuwait is Shiites, who get great support for the neighboring countries.

In addition to the tribal and ethnic consideration, money has a great influence on the electorate and votes can be "bought" on payment of money. Since the number of voters is very small, any person can win the election, if he is ready to spend for it.

There is no ideological group in those years, but the people having similar views group together to form a strong base. The liberals having majority in the assembly, stood as a strong opposition to the government and their conflict will the government forced H.E Amir to dissolve the assembly.

On the other hand the Bedouins, have lost their very low privileges and treated as stateless because majority of them supported Iraq during the occupation. There are nearly 120000 Beduins in Kuwait, who cannot work or educate their children in Kuwait. They are agitating to regain not only their old rights but also for more considerations.

This uncertain situation inflicted a kind of insecure feeling in the public, which prompted the people to invest more outside Kuwait. There is a snagging in the economy; no new project from the private sector has come up.

The remittance business of our company is improved because both nationals and expatriates transfer their income to safest haven. Still the profit margin is very high and we are the only company so far having the telex remittance facilities. The postal system starts functioning, but does not get the confidence of the public.

Life is monotonous, since the memories of the hell like situation during the occupation, haunt the public. The vibrant youngsters succumbed to fear of the future.

In the end of the year 1993, our General Manager, Mr.Gamal Zayed returned to Kuwait and stayed for one month. He returned to Cairo to continue his treatment.

He is the most indefatigable person I met in my life. One month before the Iraqi invasion of Kuwait, he was paralyzed when his blood pleasure level had broken the top level after a small verbal scramble with me. Surendra Nathan who was jealous on my contact with the top level management and the extra bugs I was getting as appreciation of my work, infuriated him saying that I was joining a commercial bank and my work should be taught to other employees, especially to his relatives. Mr. Gamal Zayed believed that and asked to hand over the duties to others. I handed over the duties and left home without teaching them. He called me the next day and gave the terminal notice and asked to teach them which I refused saying that if an employee is terminated he can leave at any time. That provoked him.

The next day our Managing director enquired the truth to the bank where I am allegedly employed and found that I never approached them for a job. He called me immediately and asked me to continue my work.
He did not forget to warn Surendra Nathan and others the consequence if they try to harass me again.

End of July 1990, Gamal Zayed was taken to Cairo for better treatment. Our MD, Mr.Abdul Razak took me to the Hospital to see Mr.Gamal off. Gamal, who could not speak held my hand and wept like a child.

But in the hospital bed in Cairo, he heard that Iraqi army occupied Kuwait and all are leaving Kuwait. He was much worried about his belongings especially his wife's gold ornaments kept in the strong shelf at his flat here. He traveled with his brother in law from Cairo to Kuwait through road to take the things. As a miracle he regained his motion and speech.

After staying one day in Kuwait, he returned on the car of his brother in law to Cairo. Only because of the air pollution in Kuwait, he refused to join in the company from the beginning.

Now he is back, I am afraid to meet him, 'what will be his attitude toward me?'

But, he came to me and said 'it was mistake. I doubt your sincerity. I must have been considered your dedication to your duties. I trusted all important work on you, not even to Nathan.'

He continued "he tried to create hatred. But I always considered you as my brother. You did a great thing when you avoid him and his set of people"

I replied "I am really sorry for what has happened. I want to protect my job. Hence I behaved like that."

He responded "I failed to recognize that time. I will be here only for 10 days. The atmosphere is still not clear. I will come again after 3 months"

Now the company is terminating and rehiring all employees. He came to collect his indemnity for the long 30 plus years' service in the company and ensure the reappointment in the same post.

He said Najeeb will come next week for a short period.

We had a short discussion about the old employees of our department, Jacob, Varghese, Kumar, Sakthi, Francise etc.

When my attempt to join a job in Kuwait University, I met several persons for a job and submitted applications to several offices. One day I met an old friend Mr. Ali, who is working in Al Muzaini Exchange Company as a Dealer. He told 'the secretary of the International department Mr. Sadeq is planning to resign from the company. He is an Iraqi and now migrating to Canada. This job is not suitable for your education, but I suggest you join now to look for another better job.'

I told "I badly need a work now for survival. So I am ready to accept this job"

'There is a problem now' he said 'the department head is one Mr. Nathan from Changanaseri. Whenever there is any vacancy, he will bring any of his relatives from India and train there for six months and find a job in any bank influencing any officer there. To reciprocate to the officer, he will hire any of the officer's man in that vacant post. All the present employees in the department joined the company in the same way.
So be careful. I will arrange it without the knowledge of him. You come to the office tomorrow 10:30 and ask me"

As agreed I reached Al Muzaini office at 10:30 AM and met Mr. Ali. He asked me to sit in visitors' room in front of the Chairman's office. After 20 minutes he guide me to the cable of the Deputy General Manager, where Mr. Sadeq is waiting for me to submit his resignation along with my job application I entered the office the Deputy General Manager, accompanying Ali and Sadeq.

I wished him "assalamu alaikkum" and he replied 'wa allakku massalam".

Then Ali explained to him the reason why we are meeting him.

The DGM is a Saudi national, named Fahed Al Misfer in his early forties who starts his questioning to me. He started 'You are highly educated. Why you choose this job. You will leave the job when you find another suitable job'.

I explained my condition and assured that I will continue to this job.

Fahed said 'that is good, you join in this job. I will transfer you when I find a suitable post'

Thus I joined the job inviting the hatred of Mr. Nathan, who does not want to waste the time of his nephew who just has appeared the final year degree examination and shows no patience for the treasure hunting in Kuwait. Alas, he can do nothing now because his request to cancel my appointment is rejected by Fahad Misfer.

On the same day and Egyptian Lawyer, Kamal Karus is also employed in a higher post on the recommendation of Mr. Gamal Zayed, then Assistant General Manager. Nathan does not like that appointment because no clear designation or responsibility is given to him and Nathan suspects that this man may be a threat to his job.

When Nathan went with Gamal Zayed for a business tour for one month, he handed over his duties to Kamal although Fahed advised him to transfer his responsibility to me. He got the support of Gamal, who said I was new in this business. Later I came to know that he took that decision because he did not want me to continue in the company.

But, God has decided a different thing that must be happened as he wishes. Kamal wrote a figure $ 5000 instead of 500 for a telex transfer, Mr. Fahed Misfer has computed the authentication key and I executed the transfer. When Fahed enquired to Kamal, he said lie to him. Fahed became angry and terminated him and transferred the work to me. Latter, Kamal was rehired to another department. Thus I got the charge of the department within 10 days after joining to supervise other staff in the department who is having working experience of 5 to 15 years. After the business tour, Nathan went directly from there to his home in India for one month vacation.

I reach the office 1 hour ahead of opening and work during lunch break to learn thing and execute the work without any mistake. The work is executed perfectly and the business is running smoothly.

When I first joined Al Muzaini Exchange in the year 1980, Jacob was on vacation for two months and he returned after his marriage. He did not like my current position and tried to grab the job from me. There also Mr.Fahad came to my rescue and ordered to obey my instructions. Thus I had a strained relation with him.

Varghese and Francis cannot agitate because of their low profile, but can side indirectly with Jacob, who is now trying to play the religious card. There are boys of Mr.Nathan; hence I always expect some troubles brewing there.

Kumar is a very quiet and intelligent person, transferred from Thomas Cook Travel Cheque office and is getting a very high salary, which is the main reason for the dislike of Jacob and others.

Kumar's father is an officer in a local bank and settled here with his second wife and children. He has divorced Kumar's mother long back due a family feud between the families of his mother and father, the main drawback of the arranged marriage system of India in olden days. Even the silly quarrel between any two members of the families will end up in divorce of the very lovely couples.

This being truth, Jacob invented a story libeling the mother of Kumar and spread in the branches. Although Kumar showed his hatred to Jacob publically, Jacob shamelessly uses his private properties and consumes the snakes and nuts brought by Kumar for his own personal uses, disregarding his objections. Not only Jacob, but his wife, who is working in another department of the same company also do the same thing, which prompt the irritation of Kumar publically. This shameless couple still continued their beggarly habit which persuades Kumar to keep his belongings at an unattainable area to them. He does not get any support from Mr. Nathan while Jacob is gathering all others against Kumar inciting communal feelings. After a short time he left the company informing the management his bitter experience in the office.

I took this as a warning to take extra care when dealing with these people and I am always expecting some kind of mischief from them. These boys are sycophants of Mr. Nathan, who publically encourage them, forgetting his official responsibility for keep the calm and quite working atmosphere. To add to the problem, he brought the son of his closest friend, Sakthidharan and architect of his posh building at Trivandrum in an unscrupulous way.

Sakthidharan is brat just passed the higher secondary school, but his father want to send to Gulf countries to keep him away from his gangster group which is involved in several criminal activities. He is not only a scoundrel but also a thief stealing things without any shame if caught red handed.

Gamal and Naguib came two times each during that year.

The company earned a recorded profit in the year 1992. Above this company earned a good compensation for the losses from UN compensation of war victims and from Kuwait Government. The company settled all his debts.

Middle of 1993 Gamal and Naguib came together prepared to work continuously. By this time, Kuwait became normal.

More exchange companies resumed their operations and everyone got telex machines. The postal system is functioning well.

One Bahrain based Exchange Company arrived in Kuwait under the sponsorship of one influential Kuwaiti citizen and got the license for exchange business. They have a home delivery system to India; the draft will be delivered at the beneficiary's home or bank in the next day morning. To market their product, they reduced the exchange margin to half fills above the Central bank USD top side rate while others were taking minimum 25 fills. There was an exodus from other company to this new company.

Since we do not start the Indian Rupee business so far, this is not affecting us now. But we anticipate a big blow when they start the business of other nations, especially Egyptian.

Now, Gamal and Naguib are idle and they want to take their responsibility back from me. They were closing watching my way of functioning and in October 1993, I handed over the charges to them. By this time, we are forced to reduce the exchange margin to the same level of other companies. This year also we will get a very good profit.

More staff joined our department and Azal is shifted to General Manager's office as his secretary, an appointment which Gamal does not like. In this metropolitan city, people like their own nationalities, then their caste and then their creed.

One day, Azal did not come to the office, next day also, and then people enquire the reason. Gamal takes this a chance to terminate her and hire an Egyptian Lady as his secretary. When he approached the M D Mr. Abdul Razak Al Muzaini, he informed him the story.

A Yemeni young man working in the office of an automobile company married Azal two days ago. He is a cheat and Azal comes to know that he has another wife at his native place on the first night itself. She wants talaq (divorce) and blamed her mother for all happened to her now.
On that night fire engulfed her mother, relieving her from all the worries. She was cooking food for the marriage feast when she caught fire, by accident. Some people say that she end her life as repentance of her mistake to investigate about this bridegroom properly, or she is hurt by the words of her daughter or from her thought that she has no aim for living after sending her daughter or the thought that she is isolated and how can she continue her life.

Now I take the responsibility to resume the Indian rupee business. With the help of one influential person, I found out the reason that prompt Reserve Bank of India refuses our applications. With the help of the same person, I succeeded to get their license.

The next job is to modernize the operation of the company. We installed all the modern business machines in the company. SWIFT system started in Kuwait, I checked their requirement. Gulf bank is the acting chair member for Kuwait and discussed the matter. They agreed to inform me when the area manager of SWIFT arrive Kuwait from Bahrain.

I have prepared all documents and have prepared a projection report to present to him when he reaches Kuwait. As expected he came to Kuwait the next week and I got an appointment to meet.

Although the banks launched the SWIFT operation before one year, they are still following the old methods to communicate with their correspondents. My projection is 200 messages per day which is higher than the total volume of banks. I also promised him that I will double it in two months time. He accepted our application under the condition; the average volume should never fall before 200 per day.

The SWIFT instruction manual is 21 books of 200 to 500 pages thick. They send the installation CD and the passwords in separate envelop. It is hilarious job to read all this books and install. With my hard work and luck, I succeeded to operate it.

The next issue is to train the staff to use it. All are enthusiastic to learn it and with a short time they became experts.

Unlike other services, SWIFT technology changes every 3 months and I spent all my extra hours for learning this.

CHAPTER 11

T HE TREAT FROM Iraq is end up after the demarcation of the Kuwait Iraq border in the year 1993 and recognition of Kuwait as a sovereign state by Iraq in the next year.

The external treat has gone, but the internal issue is raising the head to keep the tension alive.

The unity of Kuwait citizen became a myth in the past and now divided into ethnic groups; the people are fuming inside for various reasons mainly the religion.

There profit of the company showed a nose dive in the year because the changes in the business conditions of Kuwait.

Mr. Gamal Zayed is blamed for the set off in the profit of the company after three years of high profit. Even, some Directors feared that the company is going back to the pre-invasion time.

One day, we heard the shocking news that the husband of Azal left to other world leaving her and her three sons, without any protection.

He is a heart patient but never told this fact to Azal. He used to watch the TV till midnight until the children sleep. When Azal called him there was no response, then she went to him to see that he is lying in the floor dead vomiting blood.

Everyone was sympathetic to Azal and Mr.Abdul Razak asked the HR manager to pay the full salary to her during the period of Iddah,

The misfortune is following this family as heritage, from mother to daughter and then to the grand children.

In the year 1998 Tariq left the company after a dispute with Aden. Tariq is the first cousin of Adel's father and mother. He is the son of the sister of Adel's grandfather (both father of his father and father of his mother also). Above all he is the brother in Law of the Chairman. Disregarding this relation, Adel behaved very badly in front of other employees who are respecting him.

In the year June 2002, I made a short visit to home country with my family through Chennai and returned alone after four days. My family stayed in my newly built house for three months until the school reopened after the summer vacation.

All were rejoiced from the fear and all the worries of war had been buried. All start to live pleasantly and all faces bear smile of happiness. Everyone is employed and there is a salary hike recently.

Then the shocking news come that America is going to attack Iraq to destroy weapons of mass destruction. Millions of people worldwide protected this war preparation arguing that there is no clear evidence that Iraq is holding such weapons.

But, USA and UK, who helped Iraq in the early 1980s to development biological weapon to sweep away the Iranians and Khomenis who over threw their best ally in Middle East, Shah Mohamed Reza Pahlavi and converted Iran into a Islamic State, know that they are possessing such weapons. Also they are afraid that Iraq has developed Chemical Weapon with the help of some European Nations. The main worries are that these weapons may be used again Israel who is their best power grid in the Middle East and who one time bombed their Nuclear plant.

There was no U N Mandate to attack or disarm Iraq, although U N has passed nearly 60 resolutions to liberate Kuwait from Iraq. Even the Human right activist argued that the war is crueler than the depressive rule of Saddam Hussain.

On the day, 15 February 2003 when the largest ever anti war rally in Rome took place, I and friends view the protest on the TV.

First person said "After this protest the US will abandon their plan" Another said 'there is no chance for that Bush should do something to save his face at the 11 September 2001 attack of world trade center"
Third one said 'Westerners will use any opportunity to destroy the Gulf, They see the Muslims as their enemy."
Hearing our conversation one Arab joined us and said "Even the government is trying to sowing the hatred in the people. They have their own interest"

After a pause, he made a lengthy lecture on this matter. According to him, the oil wealth of the Gulf is used by USA and Western countries. They do not want to Arabs make factories, schools and other facilities because the funds deposited with then will be partly withdrawn or new funds will not come. The only way to block the funds outflow is to make confrontation among people and countries. Saddam Hussain was once a pawn in their hands. He is a stupid man who plays without thinking the consequence. Above all, westerners want the safety of Israel.

Everyone is worried that Saddam Hussain will use chemical and/or biological weapon if he is pressed to do that. There is widespread rumor that Iraq has hidden these weapons to neighboring countries including their enemy nations, Kuwait and Iran.

There is various news and propaganda about these types of weapons and the precautions to be taken to mitigate the effect of this. Several kind of mask is widely sold at very high prices. Some advised to keep coal at home and put wet coal in a cloth and cover the mouth and nose with it and pour water over it to keep it wet.

I asked my wife to go to my home in India with the children. She refused saying "if we die we will die all together. We do not go leaving you alone here".

I tried in vain to convince her, but she said that most of the people are not going and why do we go now. The schools are open now and business is going as usual.

She shows extra ordinary courage now, but I know that she will break at critical moments.

As the days are nearing she asked me to buy 3 masks for the children to protect them.
I asked her "you are very courageous, now what happened"
She replied, "I regret now to stop you to send the boys home. Chechi will look after them. Now I am afraid that they will be sick in this young age."

She calls her elder sister chechi.

I purchased 4 masks from the pharmacy on my way back home from my work. She asked me "why there is only four. Why do not you buy one more?"

I said a lie "there is only 4 available there now. Tomorrow I will buy one to carry with me when I go to office. Also I will buy on sack of coal tomorrow"

Before the war, the government authorities checked the sirens and wherever the sound of siren is heard, she starts shivering with fear. She will wear the masks herself and to the children. She is much afraid of my safety and telephones me every 10 minutes if I am at work.

All the windows are closed and sealed with sponge and adhesive tapes and the outside door is always closed and sponges pushed into the side of the door to keep it air tight. Whenever siren blows we switch off the Air conditioner and wear the mask and sit fearing the worst thing in life. Long time before the siren starts blowing and worrying the people.

On 19th March 2003, the war started amid worldwide protest of 10 million people in more than 800 cities in the world.

The Iraq military have lost their man and ammunitions due to the lengthy war with Iran and then to the First Gulf war nicked named as desert storm. More over the Iraq is isolated and financially struggling. All the soldiers are very tired and the people are fed up of the continuous wars. Despite all their fatigue, the soldiers stand behind Saddam Hussain to protest the countries from enemies inside and outside Iraq.

One day on missile crossed the anti missile shield of US troop and fell in the desert near to Air port making a ear drum bursting sound. We are all afraid and the shops and offices are closed for two days.

There was no other incident in the populous area of Kuwait for the next few days except a missile flied with heavy noise fell in the sea near the Sief Palace, frightening the whole residence of Kuwait. The people worried not only a direct hit of the missiles but the chemical or biological war head carried by these missiles.

Fortunately the war ended in the first week of May 2003, causing a war related casualties of more than 600000 people, mostly innocent civilians. Still many Arabs believe that this war is the revenge of Americans for the world trade centre attack in 11 September 2001.

Saddam Hussain was disposed in May 1, 2003 and he went on hiding.

The U.S. and allies propagated several reasons for the war and the main only is the possession of weapons of mass destruction and Saddam Hussains tie up with Al Qaeda.

Latter it is proved that all these allegations were wrong.

He was arrested on 14 December 2003 and executed in the year 2006. His heroic march to the gallows was viewed in the TV by millions and even his opponents admired him at that moment.

In the middle, another big job is entrusted to me. The company gave contract to renovate its computer systems to a software development company name, International Turnkey System (ITS) in the year 1989. The work can not be completed at that time because of Iraqi occupation. Now that company informed us that they can not complete that job, in the present situation. So, we have to find out another company.

Naturally the job is assigned to the IT Manager, but wants to do him by bringing experts from his home country, Pakistan. The management agreed to his suggestion saying that they will bear all the expenses. The IT manager has his own idea, he will not bring the people in Kuwait, but he will do the work as an outside contractor. His brother in Law was the previous IT manager and now he settled in UK doing software development work. Since the price asked by his is very high, the company asked him to find out other sources. He does not make any attempt and stick to his option, the management asked his explanation. Irritated by his replay the company terminated him. Keeping him in the chairman's cabin, another board member closed his cabin and asked to leave the office building.

Thus that responsibility falls on my shoulder. I wrote to some reputed companies in the world, two company representatives came to our office to study the requirements.

Now, Adel Muzaini has another idea, one of his friends has a small computer shop, Al Faris computers, selling locally assembled PCs. One of their employees was working with ITS before and knows software development. They planned to bring engineers from Syria and develop the program. Thus the contract is given to them.

That Syrian engineer will be present in my office each and every day to learn the work and spend daily two three hours to explain to him.

One day, he said "tomorrow I go to Canada to settle there. After completing my visa problems I will return here to complete the job"

He traveled on the day of Trade centre attack and held at USA for interrogation. We were in the US custody for several months.

So, Al Faris Company went to India and brought some computer experts. They restarted the work from where the Syrian stopped. The program lagged years and the Chairman was annoyed much.

One day he asked me in front of Adel Muzaini why I delayed the work. I said I am not handling this job, which he knows very well. He said "Now we gave them nearly 5 years. So better you find out another one and start the work from tomorrow. Do not wait for any one"

That was a Thursday and the company branches are working on Fridays in the evening while Head office is closed on Fridays. Hearing this, Adel Muzaini arranged with his friend Al Faris to install the system before completion to all branches and Head office.

I came to know the change in the system only when I reached the office on Saturday.

Since the branches are open half days on Fridays, the number of transactions is in the range of 600 to 800. The copies of all transactions are sent to me in the early morning of Saturday for further action.

This Saturday, there is no parcel from any of the branches to me which raised my suspicion.

Ramzy came to me and asked my opinion of the new program.

I asked him "why you install the system without proper arrangement"

He replied "Adel asked me to go with him. I accompanied him, but I do not agree with him. I asked him to call you, he does not want you to involve on this"

I asked him "why? I am the person who spent more time for explaining the things to the computer engineers"

He said, "He is angry to you for what you talked to the chairman. He hurried the things because of you"

I told, "Only I answered the questions of the chairman, I do not say anything extra"

"Why you offered another company to him. You don't know that Al Faris working for us" he said as if I made some crime.

I replied "the chairman asked me to find out another company. I do not contact any company for the last four years for this purpose. We talked in front of Adel.

"I don't know what is wrong with him. Now you check the system. No one in the accounts department received the log in codes" he said.

Then I noticed the two PCs kept on the two corners of the hall. In front of Ramzy, I switch on the power of one of the PCs and the system asks to key in the log in ID, which is not provided to any of us.

"What about the hard copies of yesterday's transactions. We want to process it" I asked him.

He replied "everything is on line. You need not re process it. But nobody knows how it works"

He continued 'May be some one from Al Faris come to show us"

After one hour, Akram an engineer from Al Faris computers came there and opened the system. He wants to show the operating procedures to the staff.

I asked him "first you show us the remittance system to enable us to transmit the yesterday's remittances; otherwise the customers will create problems"

When he opened the remittance menu, to our amazement we found more than eleven thousand transactions in the system, which is never exceeded 800 before on Fridays.

Ramzi said, you better send the actual one now and we will delete the duplicate items.

I asked him "how can I trace out the real one. I have not documents to verify ".

We telephoned to branches to send the hard copies of these vouchers immediately.

After 10 minutes the documents from the nearest branch are received. While I am checking the documents, Mr.Adel Muzaini came to my cabin with Ramzi.

In the first application alone I found three grave mistakes, the bank name, currency code and remittance amount, which I showed to Mr. Adel and Ramzi. I listed several mistake in the other transactions and there was not a single voucher without error.

I made a suggestion to postpone the use of the new system and continue the old system for 10 more days to rectify the errors and train the staff. Hearing my suggestion, Adel exploded saying that I had hidden agenda to bring another company.

He called Al Faris, who came with all his engineers to examine the functioning. By this time, I list the huge number of mistake seen in the applications. Since Adel explained them my attitude and my "agenda", they also suspected me. Our MD, Mr.Abdul Razak also joined the discussion and side with me, while Ramzi stood neutral. Ramzi behaved diplomatically to please both Abdul Razak and Adel.

Thus the matter is escalated to top management and the chairman interfered in this issue from Geneva. Abdul Razak asked me to list all the mistakes and give him.

Because of this incident, Al Faris refused to give log in ID to me and give the ID to my assistant. I decided to distant from this until they solve the problems.

But, in the evening of that day, they approached me for my assistance to transfer the data to SWIFT system. A technician from IT department is appointed to set up the new SWIFT terminals and I was ordered to train him.

The two staff hired for business development also shifted to the SWIFT room to monitor the function of the new system and I am cornered. I understood the challenge to my job, but kept quiet hoping they will find out their folly very soon.

Since the transfer applications are not processed for more than one week, customers start complaining. I am summoned to the office of the Chairman where all the board members, General Manager, Ramzi, Al Faris and the system developers are present.

They asked to explain the issues of the new system and I gave them the list of 116 mistakes noticed by me so far. The developers promised to rectify these errors within one week, but I must assist them in doing that. In the meantime, I must find out the real transfers and transmit to avoid further delay. I must work in the presence of the system developers and teach others to do this job. After one week AlFaris engineers brought a new version of the software rectifying some of the problems listed by me. But, in the new version there are some new errors, which are not noticed in the old version.

One developer told the other in their mother tongue that the program should be rewritten and more alteration is not possible. The tea boy who is hearing this conversation informs me this. Now they are caught and they explained me their problems which they blame on Essam, who initiated the software development but now in jail in USA. Essam has gone to half of the way, the new people continued from the place where he started without collecting the baton in their relay.

While we are discussing the matter, Ramzi came to me and joined us. I do not know what Ramzi told to Adel, who later asked the detail of our discussion. Adel also called these two engineers and enquired the matter. He showed his anger to them for telling the truth to me.

Like the adage "there will be lady behind every man's success', the normal saying in Kuwait is "there will be an Egyptian behind every Kuwait's ruin"

Adel is a very enthusiastic and hardworking young man, who is struggling to build a good image among his family members by improving the performance of the company and generating good profit. He knows that mismanagement and over ambition in the past has spoiled the company. He has good relation with me until this present issues happened.

Recent days unable to withstand the pressure due to the failure of the new system, Adel is found mentally agitated and behave arrogantly to every one

On 22 June 2004, the system stopped working in the middle of the day and the engineers cannot restart the system for a long time. Adel has joined them to solve the problem. I sat in my cabin drafting a letter to a correspondent bank without caring the events happening outside my cabin. I have nothing to do in that matter.

May be my disinterest or his believe that I know the solution for that problem, make Adel angry to me and shouts at me using obscene languages. I angry respond by saying that I do not want your job and take my personal belongings and go out of the room.
He did not expect such a behavior from me and he melted like ice cubes. He came behind me to order me to go back to my work, which was not acceptable to me. There was an angry exchange of words in front of other staff and two customers.

I came down to the front gate and telephoned to the General Manager to explain the incidence.

After some months, I heard that that computer program was abandoned and a new one is brought from a company from Dubai.

When I hung up my telephone, one customer who was watching my conversation with Adel handed over to me his mobile phone to talk to his employer. His employer is looking for a manager to run his newly opened exchange company.

I met him at 7:00 PM on that day and signed my employment contract.

That was the end of era and I left my work for the last twenty four years.

The new company is in the primitive stage of establishment, there is neither a trade license nor a shop so far. There are three other companies in Farwaniya area alone for the same owner and I got a seat in one of his companies. He has several other businesses, including a very big agricultural company with a capital of KWD 30 million. This company has 5 cargo ships to bring live stocks and vegetable from abroad to sell in all the GCC countries.

There was no salary for me for the first two months; I planned to research other job.

One night the PRO of Al Muzaini Exchange came to my residence with a stranger, who claimed to be the representative of the AL Moosa, an exchange company owner who is looking for a capable person to run his businees, because the present management of this company, Wall Street Exchange does not want to continue. I met both Mr.Moosa and the managers of Wall Street Exchange co. The relationship between these two entities are at the bottom level, and each one is blaming the other for the miserable financial condition of that company I have not interest to join that company, at the same time, I know the difficulty to find out a job at the age of 55.

Some companies from the neighboring GCC countries are biding for the purchase of this company, one of these companies is Bahrain based Zenj Exchange Company. I acquaint one of the partners of Zenj Exchange, Mr. Ali Abul, a very energetic and educated young man

And he promised a high profiled job if he can purchase one suitable business in Kuwait.

So, I started searching for any forex company that can be bought. I found out some small company struggling for working capital, but they are demanding millions for sale of their licenses.

Now the Central Bank of Kuwait increased the minimum paid up capital required from KWD 500,000 to KWD 1,000,000 for new licenses to open Foreign Exchange Company.

The present license of International Trust Group is for trading of banknotes only, which can not be transferred to the business category "Foreign Exchange Company" for doing business of funds transfers, issue of demand drafts, cheque deposit and collections, precious metals etc.

At this juncture, Nasser told me his real financial condition as his failure in the case for ownership of his main company, Saudi Kuwait Agricultural Company and his heavy loss in the Share market. Someone advised him to start a foreign exchange company, which help him to roll over a good volume of money to get relief from his financial strain.

He lost the control of the agricultural company fully and the judicial court had ordered him to pay a big sum as compensation to other partners. His father is a butcher, who imported sheep from Saudi Arabia to Kuwait to slaughter and sell through several outlets in Kuwait. Latter he joined with two Saudi suppliers to bring sheep and other livestock from countries especially, Australia and Pakistan. For that they purchased two ships in the beginning and another three when their business expanded to other GCC countries. Since the two Saudi persons are illiterate, they agreed to keep Nasser as the Managing director of the company. Actually the Nasser's father has only a nominal share while the other two rich men invested nearly the full amount. They latter came to know this truth and filed a case, which they won in all the courts.

Nasser is a naïve man, who cannot manage even one of his 22 businesses properly and his inability is used by others fully for their own benefits. He sponsors some body's business which later becomes a burden for him, because the maximum number of visas taken for these companies are sold outsider, major share of the sale proceeds go the office manager and the PRO.

From the conversation of some of the employees of that company, I came to know that all employees, especially the office manager has embezzled a huge amount

One of his cousin, who worked in the same company one day told me how he and other workers of the Agriculture company load more sheep in lorry to the market than the number shown in the gate pass and the how they share the proceeds of the robbery with the financial cum office manager.

The Financial cum office manager bought big buildings and hotels in his native country while the owners are struggling.

Still Nasser believes that man who only care about him and lie about others. Here again the sayings 'there is an Egyptian behind every Kuwaiti man' is true.

Nasser is only a doll in the hand of the Egyptian, who encourages others to embezzle funds and share with him. He is very shrewd and crooked and able to convince Mr. Nasser any untruth as truth.
One of the major businesses of Nasser is stock brokering, for which he hired a floor in the stock exchange building and invested a very high amount. Due to the world recession or God's punishment for his untrustworthy behavior he lost every thing there also.

He still believes his old employees and employed them who had no knowledge of exchange company business. Thus his old secretary becomes the General Manager of the new company while his office manager is reappointed as accountant of this company. With their advice, he has taken the license of banknotes traders, which require a very good amount of capital to run it.

Nasser has succeeded to find a shop in the best business center and furnish it. Unfortunately, he bestowed the work of the interior to his construction company who has no previous experience of exchange company set up. The counter is built in such a way that the teller has to stretch his head to see the monitor and the customer has to bend to talk to the teller. Although the fittings are costly, those are fixed awkwardly.

Before starting the operations Nasser has spent KWD 280,000 from his bank balance and rest from borrowed funds, better to say that he wasted this money, because these funds are paid for salaries and miscellaneous expense, without any return getting from it so far. He has no more funds and his borrowing capacity is also limited,

I suggested him to start the banknotes trade now at least to cover the rent and salary of the existing staff. He informed that he had given the license for banknotes trade to a Syrian National for a monthly fee of KWD 70/-. He said he will provide me a colour photocopy of that license to frame it and to keep in the shop and he will bear the responsibility for it. I know that we will never be caught because the address of our shop is shown in the license and if anyone is caught, it will be that Syrian. We hired a new person for banknotes deals and we started the business from March 1, 2005.

We start out the business with a small quantity of banknotes worth one KWD 28,500 consisting mainly US Dollars, Saudi Riyal and UAE Dirham. With this small business, we are able to generate a profit nearly KWD 1,800/—which cover the shop rent and the salaries of the three staffs including me. The expenses of the back office such as rent of the office building, salaries of Accountant & his assistant, driver etc must still be paid from the pocket of Mr. Nasser. He is struggling even to meet these expenses.

I spoke to him about a financial company who can assist us by depositing the required amount of KWD 1,000,000 in our company's account for a fees of KWD 10,000., on the surety of a cheque for the same amount plus the fees, and this cheque will be presented for the payment immediately on receipt the commercial license. He agreed and contacted the company himself and concluded the deal. Thus we succeeded to get the license on 12 July 2005.

On the day the license was received, Mr.Nasser was in Syria for family matters and I informed him over telephone that I can start the remittance business at any time. I want inaugurate the business at any time. He said "what inauguration? We already started our business. You start the business immediately"

The same day, we sent our first remittance outside Kuwait through Wall Street exchange. Fortunately, we approached Wall street exchange at a time they were looking for an agent in Kuwait for their new service named 'Instant Cash' and they agreed with us and opened an account in our name without hesitation. There is no deposit in our account, but like other money product service they allowed an overdraft of US$ 25,000 which is sufficient for a beginning.

The business was flourishing in the first three months with addition of new country business resulting a good profit of KWD 272,000 with a working capital of KWD 28,500.
Early morning, we transfer the proceeds of last day's sale through Commercial Bank of Kuwait and fax the SWIFT copy to our correspondent banks who consider this copy as a proof of remittance. At that time, two companies are floating in UAE and one company in Qatar. We remitted funds to individuals as well as brokers on behalf of the customers which are paid without delay to the beneficiary. We also introduced a door to door service to Egypt through Egyptian Commercial Bank, which was very attractive to our customer.

This extraordinary profit from the beginning is what has been dreamed by Mr. Nasser and he used to use the company funds for his other businesses, straining the working capital.

I am afraid of this malpractice of taking the funds of the customer which will definitely deter me from remitting the funds to our correspondent banks for reimbursing the payment of our remittance.

Smelling a rat, I tried to remit the funds to the very next day to cover our drawings, but Nasser kept one step ahead of me by submitting the cheques or payment orders in the previous day evening. This is the beginning of a total collapse of the company.

Fearing this situation of the company, I planned to start the business of an Education Institute with help of my youngest brother and my nephew who is presently staying with me. My brother arranged the franchise of one Indian University to run a distance learning center in Kuwait and my nephew, who was running a private college in our state, is now taking coaching classes for IELTS and English languages at my flat without proper license.

I approached a Kuwait National for sponsorship and he submitted all documents for the license of the institute. Unfortunately, the government department wants a non-objection letter from my personal sponsor, currently Mr. Nasser. I am compelled to inform my plan to Mr. Nasser and I request him for the no-objection letter to open the institute.

He insisted to take the license in the name of his daughter, who is a school teacher working in a government school in Kuwait. We prepared the documents including the budget for this institute, thus disclose to him that I have some money which I received from my previous employer as my indemnity.

After wasting my time for more than one year, he said simply "I am sorry, I can not help you in this case. I will ask my friends to arrange the license for you".

The condition of the company has deteriorated to the extent that banks are refusing to honour of drawing on them, unless we remit the funds in advance. The company has no funds to pay in advance, but he is still taking the customer funds on unavoidable circumstances.

The customers are starting to complain to police and each and every day I am called to police station as a part of their investigation. Whenever there is an order to report to police, I call Mr. Nasser on his mobile phone and he simply escape tell me that he is out of Kuwait and I settle the claim of the customer and he will settle it when he returns to Kuwait. I know he is inside Kuwait and hiding in his farm house and show his face only when the matter is settled. I used to refund the customer but I never reimbursed by Nasser. Thus, not only I exhausted my coffin but I also borrowed funds for interest from bank and private lenders at very high interest.

In meantime, I rent a complete floor of one building in Abbassiya Area and purchased computers and other accessories required for the educational institutes. I made a contract with a Kuwaiti to act as the sponsor and get the license. He brought the license after four months, by that time all my savings went astray and I become a debtor to several people. I could not start the institute due to lack of funds.

Politically and socially the Kuwait society becoming more and more open and democratic and several new constitutional amendment was made in these years the major one it the right of vote for women and to run for election.

Kuwait is divided into five constituency and 10 members of parliament is elected from each constituency.Each voter can choose four candidates. But the voting right is limited to small section of the society and more than 2/3 of the citizens have no voting right.

There is no political party in the countries, but individual candidates grouping to form an alliance for sharing the votes, most of them are bought at a very high price. Each candidate is spending millions of Kuwait Dinar to obtain four or five thousand vote to win the election. Very posh tents are built and people are feasted with most delicious foods and in the end, envelopes containing 2000 to 5000 Kuwait Dinar is handed over to them. Most of the voters go to several camps and take the full advantage of multiple voting right. From the date of declaration of election, the foods are arranged in each camp every day till the Election Day and real campaign depends on quality of food.

But, no assembly has completed it term since its inception and everyone is dissolved within 6 months due to the conflict between the members and the council of ministers. There are several issues in the society that can be resolved in a very amicable way, but some MPs take extreme stand and word 'grilling the minister' is one of the most used phrase in the assembly.
Democracy is granted to these people like flower bouquet to a monkey. They have learn merit of this system

Nasser who failed in the entire field decided to contest in the election in the year 2008 and spent millions by selling his financial instruments or borrowing from banks and friends. He failed miserably and become a bankrupt in the real sense, but reluctant to admit it.

He is over ambitious and always keeps an urge in his mind to attain a great recognition in the society.

Now we reached a stage that company must be closed for ever, there is no customer and the employees are not paid for months. I spent not only my savings of years but also borrowed funds.

Now, my elder children, twin boys have completed their higher secondary and applied for the Batchelor of Medicine (MBBS) course in a private medical college, which require a very huge fund.

I approached Mr. Nasser for my money and heard his grievance and at last told to sell the company to save him from his lenders. I started hunting for a buyer for that business.

I also borrow heavily from friends and money lenders for meeting my sons' education expenses hoping that the debts can be repaid once the business is sold.

I approached several people to buy this company and two foreign companies, Zenj Exchange from Bahrain and ARY speed remit from UAE came forward to buy it.

Mr.Ali Abul of Zenj exchange came in the morning and paid a token advance to Mr. Nasser. Same day, Mr.Praveen of ARY speed remit came in the night and concluded a contract with Nasser. ARY took the control of the business in the next day and I lost my job and money. Nasser says he hands over the business to manage it but ARY people say that they bought the company keeping Nasser as sponsor for payment of a fixed amount.

Now, I want to recover my money from the company and filed a case against the company to Ministry of Social affairs. Normally, lawyers are agreeing a percent of the claim amount if the case is won, but in my case, the lawyer is asking me to pay half of his in advance, because he knows that nothing can be collected from Mr.Nasser who is very clever to keep no tangible property in his name. I finally abandoned that case, because I will get nothing even if I won the case.

I am very scared because this deceitful man may defraud me and file a counter case against me taking the advantage that he is my sponsor. Gradually fear gripped me.

I spent most of the time in my bed thinking about my future, rarely go out. My memory started falling; moving from the bed is tardy and sluggish. I reach a condition similar to Alzheimer's decease.

One of my old friend with whom I shared a flat in Sharq over three years, met me near the ministry of social affairs, and enquired the reason for approaching the Ministry of Social Affairs. I could not recognize that man and behaved indifferently.

On another occasion, I telephoned friend to his office, and his secretary took the telephone. I failed to ask her to transfer the phone to my friend because I forget his name.

Now, what can be done at the age of 60, no savings but debtor to several people? My wife and youngest son are staying with me. I have paid the rent, school fees of my child, and expenses of my eldest children, meet the foods expenses. I retire from my job penniless and my children are still studying, my wife is housewife. What can I do now? I reached this stage after several years of hard work, to what I blame my foolishness or fate.

I tried to sell the flat I purchased in the year 2005 at the fast developing city of India, Kochi but the real estate developer is raising issues for the transfer of this property. The real estate company is in the verge of total collapse and the Managing director is arrested recently for non-payment of some of the doubts.

The only option left with me to sell my ancestral property which has reputation of several centuries as the house of the most revered family in that locality, thus destroy my own honour and prestige and embrace the extreme poverty and shame.

I spend most of my time on the bed, food is a rare luxury.

I look my image in the mirror, looking the most foolish man in the world, fuming with anger crushed the teeth, cursing and hitting the mirror to break it.